Praise for Jack Ke

"An outsider in America, Jack Kerouac was a true original."
—Ann Charters

"The wonder of Kerouac's muscular, free-form, imagistic language still astonishes. He remains an essential American mythologizer—one caught up in that backstreet world of bohemian life, before it was transformed by the harsh social Darwinism of capitalism . . . A hundred years after his birth, we still want to live that Kerouacian vision of life as one long cool stretch of highway."
—*New Statesman*

"Kerouac is more relevant than ever as we mark 100 years since his birth."
—*Guardian*

"Kerouac dreams of America in the authentic rolling rhythms of a Whitman or a Thomas Wolfe, drunk with eagerness for life."
—John K. Hutchens

"*On the Road* is the most beautifully executed, the clearest and the most important utterance yet made by the generation Kerouac himself named years ago as 'beat,' and whose principal avatar he is . . . A major novel."
—*New York Times*

"The way that [*On the Road*] is so enduring—so impervious to shifting cultural winds—seems to indicate something about how successfully it articulates a very American rootlessness . . . A hysterical elegy for threatened male freedom . . . Might be the last great American novel about masculine seduction."
—*New Yorker*

MEXICO CITY BLUES

WORKS BY JACK KEROUAC
Published by Grove Press

Dr. Sax
Lonesome Traveler
Mexico City Blues
Satori in Paris *and* **Pic**
The Subterraneans

MEXICO CITY BLUES

JACK KEROUAC

Grove Press
New York

Published simultaneously in Canada
Printed in Canada

First Grove Atlantic hardcover edition: January 1959
First Grove Atlantic paperback edition: June 1970
This Grove Atlantic paperback edition: March 2023

Library of Congress Cataloging-in-Publication data is available for this title.

ISBN 978-0-8021-6244-1
eISBN 978-0-8021-9568-5

Grove Press
an imprint of Grove Atlantic
154 West 14th Street
New York, NY 10011

Distributed by Publishers Group West

groveatlantic.com

23 24 25 26 27   10 9 8 7 6 5 4 3 2 1

MEXICO CITY BLUES

NOTE

I want to be considered a jazz poet
blowing a long blues in an afternoon jam
session on Sunday. I take 242 choruses;
my ideas vary and sometimes roll from
chorus to chorus or from halfway through
a chorus to halfway into the next.

1st Chorus

Butte Magic of Ignorance
Butte Magic
Is the same as no-Butte
     All one light
     Old Rough Roads
     One High Iron
     Mainway

     Denver is the same

"The guy I was with his uncle was
the governor of Wyoming"
  "Course he paid me back"
  Ten Days
   Two Weeks
    Stock and Joint

"Was an old crook anyway"

The same voice on the same ship
The Supreme Vehicle
     S. S. Excalibur
     Maynard
     Mainline
     Mountain
     Merudvhaga
      Mersion of Missy

2nd Chorus

Man is not worried in the middle

Man in the Middle
Is not Worried
He knows his Karma
Is not buried

But his Karma,
Unknown to him,
May end —

Which is Nirvana

Wild men
Who kill
Have Karmas
Of ill

Good men
Who love
Have Karmas
Of dove

Snakes are Poor Denizens of Hell
Have come surreptitioning
Through the tall grass
To face the pool of clear frogs

3rd Chorus

Describe fires in riverbottom
sand, and the cooking;
the cooking of hot dogs
spitted in whittled sticks
over flames of woodfire
with grease dropping in smoke
to brown and blacken
   the salty hotdogs,
   and the wine,
     and the work on the railroad.

$275,000,000,000.00 in debt
    says the Government
Two hundred and seventy five billion
    dollars in debt
Like Unending
    Heaven
And Unnumbered Sentient Beings
     Who will be admitted —
     Not-Numberable —
    To the new Pair of Shoes
    Of White Guru Fleece
      O j o !
     The Purple Paradise

4th Chorus

Roosevelt was worth 6, 7 million dollars
He was Tight

Frog waits
Till poor fly
Flies by
And then they got him

The pool of clear rocks
Covered with vegetable scum
Covered the rocks
Clear the pool
Covered the warm surface
Covered the lotus
    Dusted the watermelon flower
Aerial the Pad
    Clean queer the clear
        blue water

AND THEN THEY GOT HIM

The Oil of the Olive
Bittersweet taffies
Bittersweet cabbage
Cabbage soup made right
A hunk a grass
Sauerkraut let work
        in a big barrel
    Stunk but Good

4

5th Chorus

I am not Gregory Corso
The Italian Minnesinger —
Of the Song of Corsica —
Subioso Gregorio Corso —
The Haunted Versemaker
    King
Of Brattle Street.
In streets of snow
He wove the show
And worried in tunnels
And mad dog barked

KIND KING MIND
Allen Ginsberg called me

William Burroughs
Is William Lee

Samuel Johnson
Is Under the sea

Rothridge Cole parter
Of Peppers
Is Numbro
Elabora

If you know what I
    p a l a b r a

6th Chorus

This Thinking is Stopped.

Buddha's Secret Moonlight: — is
the Ancient Virtue of laying up
and thinking happy & comfortable
thoughts — This, which modern
Society has branded "Loafing," is
made available to people now
apparently only by junk.

Self depends on existence of other
self, and so no Solo Universal Self
exists — no self, no other self,
no innumerable selves, no
Universal self and no ideas
relating to existence or non-
existence thereof —

The Greatest, Who Has Undertaken
to Comfort Innumberable Beings

The Kind One
The Art-of-Kindness Master
The Master of Wisdom
The Great Ferryman
The Great Vehicle Being

6

7th Chorus

He Who is Free From Arbitrary Conceptions
of Being or Non-Being

The Genius of the Elephant

The Destroyer of Elephant-Trainers
    by Death

The Destroyer of Elephants by Death
The Destroyer of Death
The Destroyer and Exterminator
    of Death

Exterminator of Being and Non-Being
Tathagata
The Essence Master
The Womb
The Manifestor
Man's Made Essence
Essence's Made Man
The Maker of Light
The Destroyer of Light

8th Chorus

Mysterious Red Rivers of the North —
Obi Ubang African Montanas
    of the Gulchy Peary
    Earth —
Lakes of Light — Old Seas —
Mississippi River, Chicago,
    the Great Lakes —
The Small Rivers like Indiana,
    the Big Ones
Like Amazon.
Joliet flew.
    Alma, the River of Snowy Love
    — Amida, of Brightest
            Perfect
            Compassion

The Tamiyani Trail across
    the Everglades —

A i la ra la
    la rai la ra—

Singing breasts of women
    of earth receiving
Juicy Rivers — red earth

9th Chorus

We're all taking short cut
Through Death Valley
   The Volcanic Mountains
   And the Lizard Ice
   And the Lice of Sand
   — Lhasas of Weedblack
     Cock Rock Philtrite —
Redwoods so Huge
They climb passes by God —
   The Giant Angels
   In the Washington D C Blue Sky
   — — The Heroines of Cathedral
     Fellaheen Mexico —
Commenting on the Great Cities
   of the World,
The Blue Marvel of New Orleans
   (land a swamps)

   Ingers had done windows
      with penal Australia
too — pear Attantisatasa
   the Central Essential
     Indy Portuga
      c o i t

10th Chorus

The great hanging weak teat of India
    on the map
The Fingernail of Malaya
  The Wall of China
  The Korea Ti-Pousse Thumb
  The Salamander Japan
    the Okinawa Moon Spot
  The Pacific
  The Back of Hawaiian Mountains
  coconuts
Kines, balconies, Ah Tarzan —
  And D W Griffith
  the great American Director
    Strolling down disgruntled
    Hollywood Lane
    — to toot Nebraska,
      Indian Village New York,
      Atlantis, Rome,
      Peleus and Melisander,
      And

           swans of Balls

Spots of foam on the ocean

11th Chorus

Brown wrote a book called
The White and the Black

Narcotic City
switchin on

Anger Falls—

(musician stops,
brooding on bandstand)

11

12th Chorus

Indian songs in Mexico
(the Folk Chanties of Children
at dusk jumprope —
at Saturday Night power failure —)
are like the little French Canuckian
     songs my mother sings —
Indian Roundelays —
Row Canoe —
        Ma ta wacka
        Johnny Picotee
        Wish-tee
        Wish-tee

Negwayable

Tamayara
     Para ya
     Aztec squeaks

(ONLY THE MOTHERS ARE HAPPY)

13th Chorus

I caught a cold
From the sun
When they tore my heart out
At the top of the pyramid

  O the ruttle tooty blooty
  windowpoopies
   of Fellah Ack Ack
   Town that russet noon
   when priests dared
   to lick their lips
   over my thumping meat
    heart —
   the Sacrilegious beasts
   Ate me 10,000 million
   Times & I came back
   Spitting Pulque
    in Borracho
    Ork
    Saloons
     of old Sour Azteca

Askin for more
I popped outa Popocatapetl's
Hungry mouth

14th Chorus

And when they saw me
  Rowin my sailin canoe
  Across the lake of dreams
  In the Lotus Valley Swamp,
  And arrested me
  For the size
  Of my heart,
  T's' then I decided
  'Don't Come Back'
  They'll eat your heart alive
  Every time.
    But there's more blood
    I shed
    Outa my pumpin heart
    At Teotihuacan
    And everywhere else
    Including Turban Block,
    Lookout, Ork —
    I got more water
    Pissed in the Ocean
    As a sailor of the several
       seas
    Than Sallow's
       Aphorism
    will allow

15th Chorus

Meaning —
    I'm just an old calvert
    cross
        dead of die pork

I believe in the sweetness
    of Jesus
And Buddha —
    I believe
In St.Francis,
    Avaloki
Tesvara,
    the Saints
Of First Century
    India A D
And Scholars
    Santivedan
And Otherwise
    Santayanan
    Everywhere

16th Chorus

Santayana meaning,
    holy vehicle,
Uno —
    One Cross
    One Way
    One Cave inward
        down
        to
        moon

    Shining essences
  of universes of stars
  disseminated into powder
and dust —
        blazing
      in the dynamo
    of our thoughts
    in the forge
      of the moon

In the June
  of black bugs
    in your bed
      of hair earth

17th Chorus

Starspangled Kingdoms bedecked
    in dewy joint —
DON'T IGNORE OTHER PARTS
    OF YOUR MIND, I think,
And my clever brain sends
    ripples of amusement
Through my leg nerve halls

And I remember the Zigzag
                Original
                Mind

      of Babyhood
      when you'd let the faces
            crack & mock
            & yak & change
            & go mad utterly
            in your night
                firstmind
                reveries

      talking about the mind

The endless Not Invisible
    Madness Rioting
Everywhere

18th Chorus

The bottom of the repository
  human mind

The Kingdom of the Mind,
  The Kingdom has come.

It's the only thing you got free,
  the Mind

Per Se Williams, the critic
  and author,

Slept in a rainbow
When he discovered
the perfect accommodation
of Universal Mind
in its active aspect

 You'll have a Period of Golden Age
   Restitution of Loss
I've had all I can Eat
Revisiting Russet towns
Of long ago
On carpets of bloody sawdust

19th Chorus

Christ had a dove on his shoulder
— My brother Gerard
   Had 2 Doves
   And 2 Lambs
   Pulling his Milky Chariot.

Immersed in fragrant old
     spittoon water
He was Baptized by Iron
     Priest Saint Jacques
De Fournier in Lowell
     Massachusetts
In the Gray Rain Year,
     1919
When Chaplin had Spats
     and Dempsey
Drank no whisky by the track.

My mother saw him in heaven
Riding away, prophesying
Everything will be alright
Which I have learned now
By Trial & Conviction
In the Court of Awful Glots

20th Chorus

The Art of Kindness A Limping Sonnet
How the art of kindness doth excite,
The ressure and the intervening tear,
What horizons have they fled,
What old time's blearest dream!
But atta pressure of the Two Team,
Finding nothing to surfeit the bloated corpse,
Rabbed the Whole She bo be bang
And rounded them a Team.
Beam! Bleam! So no one cared.
Except the High Financier.
          Ah, but wine was never Made
          That sorely tongues gave grace & aid.

Because I cant write a sonnet
Does that make me Shakespeare?

There's a sonnet of the lotus
A rubicund rose
Death in a rose
Is prouder than satin
Emerald Isles
          Blest
    In the Archipelagoan
          Shore —
    Ferry's arrived.

21st Chorus

Not very musical, the Western ear
  — No lyres in the pines
    compare with the palms

Western Sorcery is Sad Science —
    Mechanics go mad
    In Nirvanas of hair
    and black oil
    and rags of dust
      and lint of flint

Hard iron fools raging in the gloom

But here's East, Cambodian
    Saloons of Air
    And Clouds Blest.
    Blakean Angel Town.
    Grove of Beardy Trees
      & Bearded Emptily —
    Expressing Patriarchal
      Authority
    To us listeners
      Of the Holy See

  Saw,
     said,
        Saved

Saved my Bhikkucitas

22nd Chorus

Saved my bhikkucitos
          for the holy hair

   that was found wanting
          in merde air —

Ninety devils jokin with me
And I'm running on the catwalk
At Margaritee
Jumping from car to car
In a 6o mile freight
Runnin up the pass maw
Tunnel Gore waited Ore
The fantastic steelsmoke
In choke mad tunnels
    of Timbercountry Calif.
where if I'd-a fell,
   I'd-a fell on peb pebbles
of sore iron grit,
      of hard put to it

Importunate fool that I was,
I raved to fight Saviors
Instead of listening in
To the Light — still a fool

23rd Chorus

CHORUS NO. 1 of
Blues in Bill's Pad

CHORUS NO. 23 of
San Francisco Blues

FOURTEEN CHORUSES
of Blue City Blues

Fifteen O Choruses
of Genu wine blues

Sing you a blues song
    sing you a tune
Sing you eight bars
    of Strike Up the Band

Eight of Indiana, eight
    of Israel,
Eight of Chubby's Chubby,
    eight of old Wardell

Yes baby, Count Blue
    Basie's fat old Chock
    Wallopin Fat Rushing
    Was a wow old saloon man

24th Chorus

All great statements ever made
    abide in death
All the magnificent & witty
    rewards of French Lettrism
Abide in death

All the Roman Sculptor
    of Heroes, all Picassos
    and Micassos and
            Macayos
            and
            Machados
and K e r o u a c o ' s —

even Asvaghosha's Glorious Statement
and Asanga's and Holy Sayadaw
and all the good and kind saints
and the divine unabstractable ones
the holy and perfect ones
All Buddhas and Dharmas
All Jesuses and Jerusalems
And Jordans and How are You's
— Nil, none, a dream,

A bubble pop, a foam snit
    in the immensities of the sea
    at midnight in the dark

25th Chorus

Dont worry about death
Once you're there
Because it is trackless

Having no track to follow
You will rest where you are
In inside of the essence

But the moment I say essence
I draw that word back
And that remark — essence's
Unspoken, you cant say a word,
essence is the word for the finger
that shows us bright blankness

When we look into the God face
We see radiant irradiation
From middleless center
Of Objectless fire roe-ing
In a fieldstar all its own

Is my own, is your own,
Is not Owned by Self-Owner
but found by Self-Loser —
Old Ancient Teaching

26th Chorus

Knew all along
That when chicken is eaten
Rooster aint worried
And when Rooster is eaten
Chicken aint worried

Because what's there to worry
What's there to grow teeth
To eat rebirth's beginningless
Meat of Eternal Comeback?

For Christ Sake stop saying
And saving your lives,
It's only one more hour
Beyond your pale light

There's no end on all sides
The saylessness, the sayless ork
        awk ah of child
        on afternoon sidewalk

Or of Hurubela Elephant Cow
        of Ant Colonies
        M'e'r y o cking
        in a moment
        of the Landscape day
        in Vast Acadian
            PureLand —
Buddha loved all sentient beings

27th Chorus

Krissake Wakeup
Nuts like Carl Solomon
A sharp Jew I know,
Say that all's already ended,
A dream a long time done.
Sit in the Bedlam high
Inside Mind listening dreaming
To the music of the time
Coming through the Aura Hole
Of Old Father Time
    Mustache on a Jimmy the Greek
                        stage

Ork, song of Nova Scotia,
    Silly, any, songs,
    Floating in the Open Blue,
    Balancing on Balloons,
        Balloons, BALLOONS,
        BALLOONS of Rosé Hope,
        balloons Balloons BALLOONS
        the Vast Integral Crap
              a
            Balloons

BALLOONS is your time
B a l l o o n s is the ending
   THAT'S THE SCENE

28th Chorus

The discriminating mind.
Discrimination is when, say,
    you're offered something
And you accept it one way
    or the other,
Not thinking of improving;
Then comes the Craft Gleam
And you look over to see
What's to be to advantage,
And find it, pouncin like a Puma,
Like a Miser Hero of Gold
                        Cellars
                    & Herring
                    in barrels,

— And you seek to achieve
    Greater satisfaction
    Which is already impossible
    Because of Supreme Reality
        and Time
And Timelessness Entire
All conjoined & arranged & finished
By Karmas of Rue
In heavenlands remote —
You suffer & you fall,
You discriminate a ball.

29th Chorus

"Man, now, you wont let me talk"
Gripes the irreligious feline cat —

That cat has no trumpet
But bubblegum to blow on

Poor sad Bhikku of the Forest
Of poor, lost little Nino

In Calles of Forever,
Streets of Old Burma,
Be saved secret wretched
Urchin brother hero
   You are protected
   By the Guardians
        of
        the
        Alone

All is alone, you dont have to talk

One Light, One Transcendental Ecstasy

If they dont understand that
In the South, it's because
All their Baptists
Have not been to Shool

30th Chorus

Tender is the Night
Tender is the Eve Star

F. Scott Fitzgerald, the Alamoan
    Huckster Crockett Hero
    Who burned his Wife Down
    and tore up the 95 Devils
    with crashes of laughter
    and breaking of glass
    in the monocled Ibyarritz
    the Little Grey Fox
    OF NEW HAVEN CONN
    via Princeton   O Sure

Tender is the marlin spike,
    Tender is the sea,
   Tender the London Fog
    That Befalls to Me

Tender is the Cat's Bath
Blue Meow
The Little Grey Fox
    That nibbled at the grapes
Tender was his foreskin,
    tender his Nape.

31st Chorus

Three Saints in Four Acts
    by Gertrude Stein
A Great Prophet
    is a Great Teacher
But he is also
    a Great Saint
And he is furthermore
    a Great Man
And more than that
    an incomparable listener
    to music and non-music
    everywhere

And a Great Sitter Under Trees,
And a Man of Trees,
And a Man of Sorrows,
And a Lemon Light
    of Angel Sounds
    and Singer of Religion
    wild singer of come-igion
    wild lover of the origin
    wild hater of hate his own

Convulsive writer of Poems
And dialog for Saints
Stomping their feet
On Pirandelloan stage

32nd Chorus

Newton's theory of relativity
    and grave gravity
Is that rocks'll fall on your head

Pluto is the Latest Star

Astronomical facts
    from under the bar.

Little cottages on hills receive
the Constellation of
the Southern Hemisphere

Where rosy doves're seen flyin
  Past Pis Cacuaqaheuro
  Monte Visto de Santo
  De Gassa — healing helium
    gas — from the substance
    on the sun star —
    gas discovered on the sun
      by spectral gazing

Sorcerers hoppity skop
    with the same familiarity
In my Buddhaland dreams —

    Monotonous monotony
      of endless grape dirigible stars

33rd Chorus

A vast cavern, huh?
I stop & jump to other field
And you wander around
Like Jap prisoners
In Salt Lake Cities
Under San Francisco's
Sewage disaster.
"An explorer of souls
and cities —"
"A lowdown junkey" —
"Who has discovered
that the essence of life
is found only in the poppy plant

with the help of odium
the addict explores
            the world anew
and creates a world
            in his own image
with the help of Madame
            Poppy
I'm an idealist
    who has outgrown
    my idealism
I have nothing to do
    the rest of my life
        but do it
        and the rest of my life
        to do it"

34th Chorus

"I have no plans
  No dates
    No appointments with anybody

So I leisurely explore
    Souls and Cities

Geographically I'm from
      and belong to that group
      called Pennsylvania Dutch

But I'm really a citizen
    of the world
        who hates Communism
        and tolerates Democracy

Of which Plato said 2000 years
        ago,
Was the best form of bad government

I'm merely exploring souls & cities
From the vantage point
Of my ivory tower built,
Built with the assistance
        of Opium

That's enough, isnt it?"

35th Chorus

It was the best show,
    the guys used to give up
    a good movie
    just to hear him talk

Now is the Time
Now is the Time
To kill an hour
    and Delaware Punch
    each

A Star is Born —
    muckle lips in the movie
    "I'd rather not" —
    "I really dont wanta go" —
    Yeah, fuck the movie.

Fuck the mambo.
Fuck is a dirty word
But it comes out clean.

  Everything (after a gasp)
  is fine, already really.
  Whatever it was.
  "Anyway it happened"
  Says Allen (Poe) Ginsberg —
  Quote from Plato right?
  Time on a Bat — growl of truck.

36th Chorus

No direction
No direction to go

Burroughs says it's a time-space
    travel ship
Connected with mystiques
    and mysteries
Of he claims transcendental
    majesties,
Pulque green crabapples
    of hypnotic dream
In hanging Ecuad vine.
Burroughs says, We have destiny,
Last of the Faustian Men.

            No direction in the void
            Is the news from the void
            In touch with the void
            Everywhere void

No direction to go
            (but)
                    (in) ward

Hm
    (ripping of paper indicates
    helplessness anyway)

37th Chorus

Mad about the Boy —
Tune — Fué —
Going along with the dance
Lester Young in eternity
    blowing his horn alone
Alone — Nobody's alone
For more than a minute.
    Growl, low, tenorman,
    Work out your tune till the day
    Is break, smooth out the rough night,
    Wail,
    Break their Beatbutton bones
    On the Bank of Broad
    England Ah Patooty
    Teaward Time
    Of Proust & bearded
        Majesty
    In rooms of dun ago
        in long a lash
        alarum speakum
        mansions tennessee
        of gory william tree
        — (remember that little
            box of tacks?)

38th Chorus

(Pome beginning with parenthesis:—
God!)
Garver has an Aztec Hammer
To batter the tacks in
It's made of Pyramid Stone
   The shape of a Knot —
   Cleopatra's Knot —
   The Knotty issue Marc
   Brandelian Antonio
   Julius Marc McAnthony
   Thorny horn of hare
   Propensities and hair
   And disgusting to the bare.
     Aztec Hammer, never stop.
    Folded ripplefold over there
        nice,
      Tacks went in,
      "It's take an artist
        to do all this"

     Careful man of cellophane
        decks
         &
       sometimes
       ceremonial
       silver foil
         but
        usually
     plain pleasant paper

39th Chorus

Comfortable Patience —
Talkin about a Hobbyman
Who draws cartoons for a livin,
Bangin in tacks carefully
For King Features Syndicate
   Has got him by the balls
   And Hammerthongs
   And central Goonyak
       Worp Ward
       Orphantail —

Aztec Stick —
     ugly Spew Smoke
     Dragon Beoryen
     smitherwolf
     Wildstar
     Monster Over the Fence
     is Frankenstein

Careful, true, Nirvana,
Patient in his Comfort,
Humble in his Demands,
Weary of the Fear,
No longer fearing
The fair happy air
Permeated with Cherub
And fingers a pair
In V Victory — meaning One

40th Chorus

Did bespat and beshit himself Rabelais,
Roundelay, singing with a chocolate
                              mouth

Did tangle in the gangles
     of legs' hair
And scream with the wine
     in his glut.

"What do you think?"

This cover is most excellent,
It's shiny and red,
This car will do nicely
All over the bed.

Rabelais was a mad nut
And also a doctor
And wrote of priests' jocks
   In 1492

Wha' hoppen in Oaxaca?

— gluts rained glut
   guts out of her
   brimy bottard
   and washed the old man's
   river underwear

41st Chorus

That other part of your mind
Where everything's refined
To thin hare screamers
Must be in the cavern
    Somewhere.

But was is its self-nature
    of location?
Nada, nadir, naparinirvana
    ni parinirvana
But Most Excellent & Wise,
  the Glorious Servant
  of Sentient Needs

Tathagata Akshobya,
    Brother of Merudhvhaga,
    Kin to Sariputra —
    Holy & Wise
    Like John in the Wood

No location to thin hare screamers
In the min   d's central comedy
        (ute
        and
        long   Nothing
        ago
        lament)
            of mind's central
                comedy   BALLOONS

41

42nd Chorus

POEM WRITTEN ON A SAILBOAT
It's a powerful sock powerful
Mock powerful breeze blowin
Across this leeward shirsh
Of fought waters thrashin
Up to spit on the deck
Of Heroing Man,
Ah, as we sail the jibboom
Upon the va va voom
And Saltpeter's her petter
Again, the Larceny Commission'll
Hear of this, fight the lawyers,
Upset the silly laws, anger
                    the
                    hare
                    brain
                    bird
                    of
                    wine
In his railroad tam o shanter
Commemorative termagant
Able to dissect such tycoon
Burpers outa their B Movies'
Investment in Black.
'Bop'
        Even on a sailboat
        I end up writin bop

43rd Chorus

Mexico City Bop
I got the huck bop
I got the floogle mock
I got the thiri chiribim
    bitchy bitchy bitchy
    batch batch
  Chippely bop
        Noise like that
        Like fallin off porches
        Of Tenement Petersburg
        Russia Chicago O Yay.

Like, when you see,
      the trumpet kind, horn
      shiny in his hand, raise
      it in smoke among heads
      he bespeaks, elucidates,
      explains and drops out,
      end of chorus, staring
      at the final wall
      where in Africa
      the old men petered
      out on their own account
      using their own Immemorial
      Salvation Mind
        SLIPPITY BOP

44th Chorus

Waves of cantos and choruses
And lilypads of anything
Like flying carpets that are
    nowhere
And all's bugged with the scene —
Ah I wish I could fight out
Of this net of mistakes
And anxieties among others
Who wait in my silence
Till I end up my work
Which never began and
Never will end — hah —
Bespeak thyself not, soft spot,
Aurorum's showed his Mountain
                  Top
Of Eastern be Western morning
  To Indicate by Moon Magic
  Constellative Stardom
        of
      Gazers
    in Mock Roman
    Arabian Kimonos,
    the lay of the pack
     in the sky

45th Chorus

Euphonism, a softening of sounds
Euphemism, a softened word —
    One is sonic, one is human
    Both are imaginary metaphors

Metaphysical Exception taken
    by the old euphonious
    phoney of Arkansaw
    River bridge

Excisor of taxes via tickets
    of taxes
With what Euphonic
    doesnt-matter
Really pronunciation
    price

Dolichocephalic?
Ichthyocephalic,
    Encephalotherapy.
    Dont point at your head
    The Judge says you're crazy
        Breaky cephalic
        Ouch
        Inch of Grace, sigh.

46th Chorus

I had a dream that Bill
G. here, was lying on his bed
talking to me in a room
in Mexico City on a
horrible afternoon, as
he mumbles information
about the crossroads of the world
I wander like a Giggling Ling
Chinese boy without rice
in a Fog Over Grass
Land vast and like life,
— in my thoughts — but
return to re-listen to what
he was saying, about loaning
money on interest, Christians,
Medicis, Churches, therefores,
Coats of Arms, Balls,
Bridge Post Pots, Guards,
I realize I am dreaming
In beginnings already
And ending's nowhere
To be seen
Yet forgotten —
Is all

47th Chorus

Where is Italy?
How can I find it in my mind
If my mind is endless.
  Skulls on the slavemarket,
    blacksmiths, doctors —
I end up bleakly giggling
    in gleak romany rooms
Sliced by Sardinian fiends
And shot fulla morphine
  By sadistic doctors
  That didnt dream of Japan
  With me the night I dreamed
  Of the Japanese Boy
  With black wool cap
  Sitting on a wall
  On Kamikaze Boulevard
  Near the Sea's Hurricane,
    In low gloomy dark
    Dusk of War 1943 —
    What happened in Italy?

48th Chorus

Marco Polo had canals
    and Venetian genitals,
In the war between Genoa
    and Venicia,
Marco Polo's was captured
And then they wrote the book
And that's all she wrote,
Because after that
    the Wandering Jesuit
    Italian Monk
    made his way to the wall
    in the China — far
    in the Indes of the
            Saints,

far in the cave of reality
down the suicide steps
into underground caves
where worshippers
like Ignatius Loyola
and the Hearer & Answerer
of Prayer, Samantabhadra,
what's his Indian name,
preside
    (like before they were born)

49th Chorus

They got nothing on me
    at the university
Them clever poets
    of immensity
With charcoal suits
    and charcoal hair
And green armpits
    and heaven air
And cheques to balance
    my account
In Rome benighted
    by White Russians
Without care who puke
    in windows
Everywhere.

They got nothing on me
    'Cause I'm dead

They cant surpass me
'Cause I'm dead
And being dead
  I hurt my head
  And now I wait
  Without hate
  For my fate
  To estate

50th Chorus

Maybe I'm crazy, and my parts
Are scattered still — didnt gather
Em when form was passin out
The window of the giver,
So I'm looking for derangement
To bring me landward back
Through logic's cold moon air
Where water everywhere
Appears from magic gems
And Asphasiax the Nymph
    of India by the Sea
  Dances princely mincing
     churly jargots
  In the oral eloquent air
    of tents'
  Canopied majesty,
    Ten thousand Buddhas
    Hiding Everywhere —
    How can I be crazy
    Even here?
        — or wait
        Maybe I'm an Agloon
        doomed to be spitted
        on the igloo stone
        of Some North mad

51st Chorus

America is a permissible dream,
Providing you remember ants
Have Americas and Russians
Like the Possessed have Americas
And little Americas are had
By baby mules in misty fields
And it is named after Americus
Vespucci of Sunny Italy,
And nobody cares how you hang
Your spaghetti wash
On the Pasta Rooftops
Of Oh Yawn Opium
Fellaheen Espagna
Olvierto Milano
   Afternoon, when men
   gamble & ramble & fuck
   and women watch the wash
   with one eye on the grocer boy
   and one eye on the loon
   and one eye
      in the universe
       is Tathagata's
        Transcendental
         orb of balloon

52nd Chorus

I'm crazy everywhere
Like the guy sailed on that ferry
        for 3 years
Between Hong Kong & China —

The British shoulda given him
        temporary residence in Hong Kong;
        but they didnt want any part
        of him first place he didnt
        have any money

Citizen somehow
    of a country behind the Iron Curtain
    Ex-Spy from Skid Row

I'm crazy everywhere
        like Charlie Chaplin
        dancing in moral turpitude
        playing Bluebeard killer
        on satin asskiss couches
        with itchy mustache
        so well known to dreamers
        of Choice's Century

Every one of us Roman Circus
        sacrifices, every one,
Returned for payment
        In America Madhouse

53rd Chorus

Merrily we roll along
Dee de lee dee doo doo doo
Merrily merrily all the day

Roll along, roll along,
O'er the deep blue sea
        "Yes, life woulda been
          a mistake without music"
        Most primitive thing we know
        About man is music, drums —
        first thing we hear — drums,
        fifes, reed instruments —
        naturals — catgut violins
        and heavenly lyres
        and along that line
        what the hell's the name
        of that instrument
          the Aeolian Lyre
          by the Sea

The Organ they made too —
Demosthenes listened by the sea
    with a rock in his teeth
And complained when he spent
    more on bread than wine —
S h h h says the Holy Sea

54th Chorus

One night in 1941 I was a kid
And ran away from college.
And took a bus to the South
Where bedbugs got in my hair
In the Heatwave Night
And all I saw on the long
Avenue were Negroes

Once I went to a movie
At midnight, 1940, Mice
And Men, the name of it,
The Red Block Boxcars
Rolling by (on the Screen)
   Yessir
        life
            finally
                gets
                    tired
                        of
                            living —

On both occasions I had wild
Face looking into lights
Of Streets where phantoms
Hastened out of sight
Into Memorial Cello Time

55th Chorus

When I was in the hospital
I had a big fat nurse
Who kept looking over my shoulder
At the book I was reading,
'The Brothers Karamazov,'
By Gambling Man Fyodor
     Dostoevsky
Of Czarist Russia, a Saint,
And in the chapters
     called Pro and Con
She kept giggling & insisting
That Pro meant Prophylactic
     and Con Contraceptive
In all her laughs & gestures.
     Of this Holy Nurse
     I learned bed wet
     comforts of hot water
     and senile satisfaction
     'I'll Take You Home Again Kathleen'
     Sang the old white Cancer man
          in the corner
     when the children guitared
          at my footbed,
     Kolya Krosotkins
          of my railroad

56th Chorus

At another hospital
I almost died
With ecstasy
Glancing at the Babylonian
Rooftops of the Bronx,
And at my fellow

Kaiser was dying of Leukemia,
Not enough thick blood,
    I had too much.
I was dying of die-sadness,
Others had diabetes
        like my Uncle John;
Others had sores in the stomach,
        ulcers, worriers? —
Sexfiends I'd say.

Old Italian Fruiterer
Had Banti's Awful Disease,
        the bloating of the belly
        by undigested water
        come from food,
        everything he ate
        turned to water.

57th Chorus

Green goofballs,
Blue Heavens,
Sodium amythol,
Sleeping compound.

Thirty of em
To commit suicide —
Lethal dose is 30 to 50
Times the therapeutic dose,
The therapeutic dose is une —
Take thirty to be safe —
Or else praps forty be better —
If you take too many
You throw em up —
     You gotta let alone
     Your stomach, if you
     threw it right down
     you would throw it up
     then, in lethal powder
     form

Better to eat the capsules
Swallow about six at a time,
Take em with cold water,
Till you get about 35 in ya
And then lay down on your back

58th Chorus

All about goofballs,
    all about morphine,
    so I read all about it,
    that's what it said,
    'Lethal dose is 30 times
    the Therapeutic dose'

Very painful death, morphine
    or heroin; never
Try to kill yourself with
    heroin or morphine;
It's a very painful death.

Doctor gave me a mainline shot
Of H grain — Jesus I
thought the whole building
was falling on me —
went on my knees, awake,
lines come under my eye
I looked like a madman
In 15 minutes I begin
    to straighten up a little bit
Says "Jesus Bill I thought
    you was dead
A goner, the way you
    looked
When you're standin there"

59th Chorus

Then I always manage to get
     my weekly check on Monday,
Pay my rent, get my laundry
     out, always have enough
Junk to last a coupla days

Have to buy a couple needles
     tomorrow, feels like
Shovin a nail in me

     Just like shovin a nail in me
Goddamn — (Cough) —

For the first time in my life
I pinched the skin
And pushed the needle in
And the skin pinched together
And the needle stuck right out
And I shot in and out,
Goofed half my whole shot
On the floor —
     Took another one —
     Nothin a junkey likes better
     Than sittin quietly with a new shot
     And knows tomorrow's plenty more

60th Chorus

C i l
Rubberbands Seventyfivedollars
I came out of the dream
That time with mind made
Of misery and tried to remember
                    the member
                    of the ball
                    who it did seem to me
                    was the most proficient
                    at devaluating the advance
                    of my profit & loss
                          company, Holmes —
                          Whatever that means

It means that I have been asked
To receive a brother
Who sinned against me
And I knew all the time
The Saints were for me.

The Saints are still for me,
      are Still,
C h i c o ,
      small angels,
   I am still for them
   I got eyes of Avalokitesvara

61st Chorus

And all my own sins
Have been forgiven somewhere —
I dont even remember them,
I remember the sins of others.

Let me meditate on my sins.
    (Judgment Gate, somebody
    stuck a spear
    through the heart
    of the Judgment Gate)
      (with her surl of leer)

    and that's how we got in

Powerful Tea you gotta smoke
    to believe that

About the actual honey
    of women's limbs

Archangels have true eyes —
They look sideways at you
And make you excise
The end from the tax bit
    of your doubts —
'S all about angels' sins

62nd Chorus

A warrant for arrest
Is a mandate,
An order from the Court
Or from the Roayal Coart
Or from the Royal King
Or from
  the Royal Coast,
  or Coat of Arms,
  or Charms,
  Boudoirs,
  Histories by Voltaire,
  Arrested disorderly
   Louis Ferdinand Celine's
   of South Africa

  murderous intelligent

If you got a lot a money
 You're a felon
If you got not but little money
 Misdemeanor

Mal-Hishaps-Deameaning
Lost Ass-Kicked Out
 or go to jail
 Keep the door locked

63rd Chorus

Rather gemmy,
    Said the King of Literature
Sitting on a davenport
    at afternoon butler's tea.

Rather gemmy, hm,
Always thought these sonnets
Of mine, were rather gemmy,
As you say,
            pureperfect gems
            of lucid poetry

Poetry being what it is today

Rather gemmy, I concluded,
    thinking you were right —
It isnt my fault that Buddha
    gave me helmet
Of Right Thought, and indices
    of long Saints
To Cope my Lope along
    with,
Seeing I never had harm
    from anything
But a Heavenly Farm.

64th Chorus

I'd rather die than be famous,
I want to go live in the desert
With long wild hair, eating
At my campfire, full of sand,
Hard as a donut
Cooked by Sand
The Pure Land
    Moo Land
    Heavenland Righteous
    sping
    the thing

I'd rather be in the desert sand,
Sitting legs crossed, at lizard
High noon, under a wood
Board shelter, in the Dee Go
Desert, just west a L A,
Or even in Chihucha, dry
Zackatakies, High Guadalajara,
— absence of phantoms
    make me no king —

rather go in the high lone land
of plateau where you can hear
at night the zing of silence
from the halls of Assembled

65th Chorus

To understand what I'm sayin
You gotta read the Sutras,
The Sutras of the Ancients, India
Long ago, when campfires at night
Across the Rahuan River
Showed lines of assembled bo's
With bare feet bare the naked
Right shoulders of passing houris,
Sravasti late at night, tinkle
Goes the Indian Dancinggerl —
   There's One Thousand
   Two hundred and fifty
   Men
   Sitting around a grove
         of trees
   Outsida town
        right now

    With Buddha
     Is their leader
      Discoursing in the middle,
      Sitting lotus posture,
      Hands to the sky,
       Explaining the Dharma
       In a Sutra so high

66th Chorus

Dharma law
    Say
  All things is made
        of the same thing
      which is a nothing

All nothings are the same
        as somethings
        the somethings
        are no-nothings,
        equally blank

Blank
    bright
        is the whole scene
      when you let your eyes
      wander beyond the mules
    and the fields and carpets
    and bottles on the floor
    and clean mahogany radios,
dont be afraid
the raid hasnt started
panic you not
      day the better
      arriveth soon
And the gist of it Nothing-ness
    SUCH-NESS

67th Chorus

Suchness
Is *Tathata,* the name,
Used,
        to mean, Essence,
        all things is made
        of the same thing
        essence

The thing is pure nature,
        not Mother Nature

The thing is to express
the very substance of your thoughts
        as you read this
is the same as the emptiness
        of space
        right now

and the same as the silence you hear
        inside the emptiness
        that's there
        everywhere,
        so nothing in the way
        but ignorant sofas
        and phantoms & chairs,
      nothing there but the picture
      in the movie in your mind

68th Chorus

My disciples of the modern world.
Christ was born in a barn because
the inn was full. Egyptian,
Babylonian, African. They
met in the desert and saw
the star and God was
s'posed to have spoken to em
— picked up.
   Like wild.
        A hayloft in a barn.
     All will appeal
     to Slaves
  Every saint of Christ
       was the guilt of slaves
  Inherit the Earth, O
      Camel thru the eye
     of a needle
  Rich man full of heaven
      follow me
      Poor
  Never die.

69th Chorus

Mary
Who's my mother?
   Goes back to Isis

Who *is* my mother?
   Christ said — You are
   all my mothers.
      All my brothers
        and sisters.
      Peace.

      The faith
          and belief
              in him

That
      through their faith
          eyes of God —
But the Catholic Church
      S hw vass iss?

70th Chorus

Who *is* my father?
Who is my mother?
Who is my brother?
Who is my sister?
I say you're all my father
            all my mother
            all my sister
            all my brother

    "Rather a good thing"
    — that we're all
    brothers & sisters
Men Of Good Will
is Something we Need
in the World Today

    Men of Philosophy
            that Cannot be of Good
            Will
            Are the Communists
            & Fanatical Jews

71st Chorus

Fanatical spews
Fanatical mews

It is magic
That men have anything
    to do with birth

Say the Primitives.
"I never objected to the word
    God"

The crazy sex
    the Protestant has

They're Brigham Me Young
God hid some tablets
    full of Gold Heroin
In the Mormon Bible

And flew pigeons & cocks
    W e l c o m e H o m e

72nd Chorus

The higher criticism
If you know what I mean
   "Literary Criticism?"
   "No — Bible."
Every chapter & phase
   Historical, anthropological,
     Archaeological, Logical,
      Magical,
     There's not after they
     get thru with the Bible
     Much of it Left

   Mo the Span
      Pure Boy

   I must n a w
      remember

Na o

73rd Chorus

The Book of Pluviums
"You want some coffee
    before I get it too good?"
A O Kay,
Straighten me out.
Z a r o o o m o o o
    (The Bus outdoors)
and he-hey the
        Nay Neigh
        of the Heaven
        Mule
            Nice clean Cup
            Mert o Vik lu
            Nut — upanu. ⸙
        Yes
        Sir.
        Merp.
        HOOT GIBSON

74th Chorus

"Darling!"
Red hot.
That kind of camping
I dont object to
unless it's kept
within reason.

"The coffee is delicious."

This is for Vidal

Didnt know I was
a Come-Onner, did you?
   (Come-on-er)

I am one of the world's
Great Bullshitters,
Girls

Very High Cantos

75th Chorus

But cantos oughta sing

HE WAS AN
OLD CROOK

The hand of death
Wrote itself

Jumping over the moon
With a Cow and Jesus

Now Onions, chickens,
Noodle end of it

Mo

Not too many hands
    of death
In slave Arabia
    the post hot
Top town
    of
        Thieves

75

76th Chorus

A GUY'S ASKING A QUESTION
It's better not to wake them up
So they wont know
They're dreaming?

It's better to wake them up
        because
        they're dreaming.

It's not better to wake them up
        because they dont know
        that they're dreaming?

Who, no, who said I
        was dreaming?

You said, who said, I say
You're dreaming?

Lise is a fl dreamy
        phantasm

"Go on, you're having one big dream,
That would be my answer." (Bill)

77th Chorus

"Dreery my dear"
  The time we crossed Madrid
   in a car
    and Kelly pointed out
    the dreary Spanish
     Ar chitecture
     As they OO'ed
     And aa'ed
     In a hired
      Li mousine
      Of the Zara
    Nazarenes
      smiling to be bold
       in foretold of old
        And they stopped
        At a balcony

78th Chorus

A Porte Corrière
Of Spanish
Portugy
Blazed
By guitars
Like Spanish Cows
Ortega y gassa
   Monte de eleor
  De manta
    Moda
   Fawt
      Ta caror
      Ta fucka
     Erv old
        Men

79th Chorus

Story About What?
 (Story About Babyhood)
 While walking down
          the boulevard
 Contemplating suicide
 I sat down at a table
 And much to my surprise
 My friend was goofing
          at a table
 And he was goofing out loud
 And this is the result
 Of what he Said.

Take your pick

Winds up in such
A predicament
You won't know
What to do with yourself
Live or die

80th Chorus

GOOFING AT THE TABLE
"You just dont know."
"What dont I know?"
"How good this ham n eggs
          is
"If you had any idea
          whatsoever
How good this is
Then you would stop
          writing poetry
And dig in."

"It's been so long
   since I been hungry
   it's like a miracle."

   Ah boy but them bacon
   And them egg —
   Where the hell
        is the scissor?
SINGING:— "You'll never know
just how much I love you."

81st Chorus

Mr Beggar & Mrs Davy —
Looney and CRUNEY,
I made a pome out of it,
Havent smoked Luney
      & Cruney
In a Long Time.

    Dem eggs & dem dem
    Dere bacons, baby,
    If you only lay that
        down on a trumpet,
      'Lay that down
          solid brother
      'Bout all dem
          bacon & eggs
    Ya gotta be able
         to lay it down
         solid —
    All that luney
        & fruney

82nd Chorus

Fracons, acons, & beggs,
Lay, it, all that
    be bobby
    be buddy
I didnt took
    I could think
        So
    bepo
      beboppy

      Luney & Juney
      — if —
      that's the way
        they get
      kinda hysterical

Looney & Boony
Juner and Mooner
Moon, Spoon, and June

83rd Chorus

Dont they call them

cat men

That lay it down
with the trumpet

The orgasm
Of the moon
And the June

I call em

  them cat things

"That's really cute,
    that un"

William
Carlos
Williams

84th Chorus

SINGING:—
By the light
   Of the silvery moon
   I like to spoon
   To my honey
   I'll
   Croon
      Love's Dream

By the light
   Of the silvery moon
   We'll O that's the
   part I dont remember
   ho ney moon —
     Croon —
       Love —
         June —

        O I dont know
        You can get it out of a book
        If the right words are
           important

85th Chorus

Do you really need
the right word
Do you really need
Of course it's all asinine
   Forms of asininity
     Once & for all

Mr. William Carlos
     Williams

Anyway,
    An asinine form
    which will end
    all asininity
    from now on

That's a poem
The poem
Will end
Asininity

86th Chorus

Take your pick,
If you wanta commit suicide.
So that we'll know
What it woulda been
   like without life.
Woulda been like
Peaceful and Golden.

A Crashing Movie
   The world
   Full of beet skins
   And fist stars
   And editorial
   Poon yaks.
A crashing movie
   The World
Full of craze
      Beware
      The Share
      is Merde
      Air

87th Chorus

These things in a big structure of Confession —
And "Later" — "Later the Road" —
Or "On the Road" simply. New
Haven Railroads of the Night
Couldnt be Tighter, than Slaw,
The Riverbottom Rog Man, Screaming
In the Passaic Rocks ready to throat
And drown the sodden once-dry dog
In a multifarious Pool of Pearls
Containing Amethystine Paradises
And Worlds a Hundred Million in Number
Fit for the following Kings:
Ashapur, Parteriat, Klane,
Thor, Mordelowr, Power,
Thwatmalee, Rizottle the Bottle
The Funny King of the Aisles —
     Ah the insane —
Make it a great story & confession
Of all the crazy people you've known
Since early Nineteen Fifty One,
In the Twat and the Twaddle
Of the Lovegirl Marriage.

88th Chorus

"I wanted to marry a lovegirl,
A girl-only-interested-in-love girl,"
that would be the first sentence
        of this masterpiece
Of golden litteratur —
        Brap. All the crazy people
        I've known since I was 4 years old
    — 6 years old I saw the sun red
        on windows of snowy centralville,
        and wondered "Who am I?"
        with truthful little eyes
        turned to the skies of paradise —
        no answer came.

I was the first crazy person
I'd known.

Had bundles and scarves a hundred miles
                                    long
Wrapt in my heart of the library,
I had bottles and barts, & Xmas Trees,
and every thing known to man,
including 6 year old ache pains
in the Poxy back.
            Was afraid of myself simply,
            And afraid a everyone else.

89th Chorus

Remembering my birth in infancy, the coughs,
The swallows, the tear-trees growing
From your eyeballs of shame; the grey
Immense morning I was conceived i the womb,
And the red gory afternoon delivered
                              therefrom.

Wow. I could sing you hounds
        make you bell howl packs,
Zounds, I'd-a lived & lived laughing
        as a child
If somebody coulda told me
        it was unreal:
I was scared. The dark
        was full of phantoms
Come from the other side of death
        to claim the hearts
Of Sacrificial little children
        laying up in the winter night
In cribs by howling windows
        of the cold & forlorn
Earth of Massachussetts February,
        Massachussetts March,
Wild howl Lupine Cold the Moony
        and Loony nights.

90th Chorus

I thought I was a phantom,
    me, myself,
Suffering. One night I saw
    my older brother Gerard
Standing over my crib with wild
    hair, as if he had just
    pee-visited the pail
    in the hall of snores
    and headed back for his room
    was investigatin the Grail,
    Nin & Ma's bedroom,
    Who slept in the same bed
    and in the crib alongside.
    Oily is the moment so
    that phantom was my brother
    only in the sense that cotton
               is soft,
    Only in the sense that
      when you die
        you muffle
          in your sigh
            the thorny hard
              regret of rocks
                of life-belief.
I knew, I hoped, to go be saved.

91st Chorus

If that phantom was real
And wanted to hurt me, then,
All I had to do was suffer & die,
Gritting my teeth awhile
Till it's all over.
If the phantom was unreal
And was only a friendly shade
Standing commiserating compassionately
At my side as I slept and sighed
In the Shakespearean night,
Perhaps, may be, it was my brother.
And my brother didnt seek to hurt me.
  If he did, I crashed,
  I saw stars, marvels,
  My miracle hullabaloo
  Balloon Rainbow
  Turned out to be "Bone
  the Brother-Crash" —
  You get socked on the jaw
  By your best friend —
  You keep thinking
  It's going to happen
  And it never happens,
    Pow!

92nd Chorus

It was all right,
And I was the strangest creature
    of them all.
At Xmas they brought me a toy house
    in and out of which
    Caroline my sister
    played little valentine
    armies showing little sad
    people of the prime
    pip Vienna smalltoot
    towns, with orchestras
    of the square,
    and in the brown light
    of the kitchen I wondered

"What is this? — mystery of little people.
Is each one a frightening as me?
Is each one afraid as me?
Is each one got to sleep
    in the dark at night?
Did any of them lil cardboard soldiers
See the Sun of Sadness at Six
In the windows of their snow slope?"

93rd Chorus

But I knew they hadnt.
They hadnt thought such thoughts.
No — I knew.
I knew I knew I knew.
It was like the Lankavatara
                    Scripture
I got to read 30 years later,
It said: "These little cardboard
Houses and people, may be real,
Considered as real, if you steal
Little reel from the wheel
Every neel till the eel
In the skeel keep the weal
 Of all men intact in city
                    halls
Of poop hope.
            In other words, son,
            hang on — dont tip,
            lose balance, see reality
            in images like cardboard
            — nor in the brown light
            of this very kitchen."
            I pouted in my childhood.

94th Chorus

But now I will describe
The crazy people I've known.
These things.
       My mother would take us
       To a three story tenement
       on Lakeview Avenue, still
       standing there — washlines
       of Araby hung from ropes
       on the brown porch —
       spend all day in there
       talkin & gossipin —
       lockin and rossipin
and plopperin and
dopperin and sopperin —
— it's easy to go crazy
I go crazy sometimes.
Can't get on with my story,
write it in verse.
       Worse
       Aint go no story, just verse
It was a crazy place to take us, I mean

95th Chorus

It was where I learned to say "door"
Meanwhile a thousand things
Were happening in the Maldoror wood
Of our neighborhood, Beaulieu Street
Up ahead, with rats of rat winery
And pestils and poolsharks
And pests of tenement crooners,
Looners — the dreary population
   Of the world in 1924.
     Two years old, I sat on the sidewalk
     Contemplating time in white sand,
     That was up on Burnaby Street.
         Names of Silly Streets.
         We have a meet to keep.
"Simplificus? Ridiculous?
 Immensicus? Marvailovous!"
The wild a thousand and one thousand
            things
  To do & be done
     when you're a kiddy
     of two or four
     in the bright ball
     inside your mind
     of heaven given
     joy.

96th Chorus

I tumbled down the street
On a tricycle, very fast,
I coulda kept going
And wound up in the river,
— Or across the trolley tracks
And got cobble mashed
And all smashed so that later on
I cant have grit dreams
Of Lakeview Avenue,
And see my father die,
Had I died at two —
    But I saw my father die,
    I saw my brother die,
    I saw my mother die
   my mother my mother my mother
         inside me —
Saw the pear trees die,
    the grapes, pearls, penny trees —
Saw little white collar girl
    with little black dress
And spots of rose on each cheek,
    die, in her glasses
In a coffin.
    But I raced my bicycle safely.

97th Chorus

Meanwhile there's my Pa, alone in street,
Coming for supper, under heaven bleak
The trees of March black twigs
Against the red & gory sundown
That blazed across the River
sinking in the ocean to the East
beyond Salisbury's latest & last
                    grain of sand,
Then all's wet underneath, to Eclipse
(Ivan the Heaven Sea-Ice King, Euclid,
Bloody Be Jupiter, Nucleus,
Nuclid, What's-His-Name — the sea
The sea-drang Scholar with mermaids,
Bloody blasted dadflap thorn it
— N e p p y   T u n e —)
All's wet clear to Neptune's Seat.
        Sensing the aura, the news
        Of that frost, my father
        Hurries in his Woe-Street
        Conscious he is a man
        Doomed to mortal destiny.
    "And my poor lil Ti Pousse,"
        he thinks of me,
    "He'll get it too."

98th Chorus

My father loves me,
    my mother too,
        I am all safe,
            and so are you.

My father adores me
    thinks I am cute
        hates to see me
            flash sheroot

Or bespatter bedspreads
    with mule of infant
        woodsy odors —
            blash aroot

My old man's only 28 years old
And is a young insurance salesman
And is confidently clacking down the street
And chuckling to think of the boys
And the poker game and gnaws
His fingernails worried about how fat
He's getting, "no coal bill's been
Highern this 1924 coalbill
I got to watch my dollars
Pretty soon the poorhouse" —
    ("Wish I was God," he adds to think)

99th Chorus

My father, Leo Alcide Kérouac
Comes in the door of the porch
On the way out to downtown red,
 (where Neons Redly-Brownly Flash
An aura over the city center
As seen from the river where we lived)
— "Prap — prohock!" he's coughing,
    Busy, "Am," bursting to part
    the seams of his trousers with power
    of assembled intentions.
                "B-rrack — Brap?"
(as years later GJ would imitate him,
"your father, Zagg, he goes along,
 Bre-hack! Brop?" Raising
     his leg, bursting his face
          to rouge outpop huge mad eyes
          of "big burper balloons
          of the huge world")
To see if there's any mail in the box
My father shoots 2 quick glances
Into all hearts of the box,
No mail, you see the flash of his anxious
Head looking in the void for nothing.

100th Chorus

That's the porch of the Lupine house.
Afternoons I sleep upstairs,
In the sun, on the porch, in October,
    I remember the dry leaves
      in the blue sky.
I remember one day being parked in the
                    wickerbasket
Baby carriage, under huge old tree,
In family photos we've preserved it,
A great elm rising from dust
Of the little uphill road —
By dry hedges on a late afternoon
In November in the North, sun warm
But air cold, I am wrapt
And beswallered in sweet ebony
With wraps and puffcream caps
And chinkly pinkly pink baby,
Gleering at the world with little
                  wet lips,
Glad, Ah John,
— that tree is still standing
but the road has moved over.
    Such is the might of the baby
        in the seat
      He hugens to re-double
      the image, in words.

100

101st Chorus

We strove to go to movies
And re discover the happiness
    of the baby —
We built up towers of prayer
    in ivory and stone —
Roused denizens from their proper
    rat-warrens —
      "Simplificus the baby,
      what hast thou thought,
      should he be serried
      and should we be clobber
      the agent of the giant
      in the picture?
           or let him guess?
             I say, let's
             let him guess.

Then he'll come crying
    & sneaking thru the tent
      looking for the showing
        of proud discontent,
          the circus of mirkus,
            pile it on thick,
            — befriend —
            it's a show to go to movies
            but a blow the baby be"

102nd Chorus

"See to it that he never ends,"
    they might have added anyhow.

One never dies,
    One's never born
        So sing the optimists
Of holy old religion,
    trying to assuage —

Your shoes may look nice,
    your baby buggies neater,
        but one dies,
            one's born.

What the Tathagata of Buddhism
                preaches,

The Prophet of Buddhahood
    is that
    nothing
    is really
    born nor dies

    But that Ignorance is its Prince,
    The essence never moved
    From folded magnificence.

103rd Chorus

My father in downtown red
Walked around like a shadow
Of ink black, with hat, nodding,
In the immemorial lights of my dreams.
For I have since dreamt of Lowell
And the image of my father,
Straw hat, newspaper in pocket,
Liquor on the breath, barber shopshines,
Is the image of Ignorant Man
Hurrying to his destiny which is Death
Even though he knows it.
        'S why they call Cheer,
        a bottle, a glass, a drink,
        A Cup of Courage —

Men know the mist is not their friend —
They come out of fields & put coats on
And become businessmen & die stale
The same loathsome stale death
They mighta died in countryside
        Hills of dung.
My remembrance of my father
        in downtown Lowell
        walking like cardboard cut
        across the lost lights
is the same empty material
as my father in the grave.

104th Chorus

I'd rather be thin than famous,
I dont wanta be fat,
And a woman throws me outa bed
Callin me Gordo, & everytime
                    I bend
                    to pickup
                    my suspenders
                    from the davenport
                    floor I explode
                    loud huge grunt-o
                    and disgust
                    every one
                    in the familio

        I'd rather be thin than famous
        But I'm fat

Paste that in yr. Broadway Show

105th Chorus

Essence is like absence of reality,
Just like absence of non-reality
Is the same essence anyhow.

Essence is what sunlight is
At the same time that moonlight is,
Both have light, both have shape,
Both have darkness, both are late:

Both are late because empty thereof,
Empty is light, empty is dark,
    what's difference between emptiness
    of brightness and dark?

What's the difference between absence
Of reality, joy, or meaning
In middle of bubble, as being same
As middle of man, non-bubble

Man is the same as man,
The same as no-man, the same
As Anyman, Everyman, Asiman,
        (asinine man)
Man is nowhere till he knows,

     The essence of emptiness
     is essence of gold

106th Chorus

Man is nowhere anyway
Because nowhere is here
And I am here, to testify.

Nowhere is
    what nowhere was

I know nowhere
More anywhere
Than this here
Particular everywhere

When I fell thru the eye of the needle
And became a tumbling torso
In the Univers-O,
                    Brother, let me
                            tell you,
                    I thought
                    I was moving
                    from somewhere
                    to everywhere
                    but nothing moved
                    so I musta been
                    and still be
                    (must) no
                    where be
        But that's all up to the Saints
I aint gonna say the Saints of Innisfree

107th Chorus

Light is Late
        yes
                because

it happens after you realize it
        You dont see light
        Until sensation of seeing light
        Is registered in Perception.

Perception notifies Discrimination,
        etc., Consciousness

Until then there was no light
So light is late

Darkness is late
        You dont conceive of darkness
        Till you've been late with light
        When you learned difference
        Between equal poles abright
        with Arbitrary i d e a s
        About somethin bein this
        Or that, abiding in this abode,
        Denying in that abode —
        Equal, positive, electric shock,
                coil, dacoit, tower,
        oil — it's all late

108th Chorus

Neither this nor that
    means,
        no arbitrary conceptions,
        because if you say
        arbitrarily, the RAMMIS
        is the RAMMIS, ! —
        and the TSORIS is the TSORIS,
        or the FLORIST,
        or the —
            arbitrary conceptions
            have sprung into existence
            that didnt have to be there
            in the first place
            when your eyes were bright
            with seeing emptiness
            in the void of holy sea
            where creatures didnt
            abound, nor crops grow,
            and nothing happened,
              and nobody lived,
              and nobody cared —

        You didnt need
        arbitrary concepts there
        and need them now
        you say you need them now
        I say, you say,
        Why should you need them now
        Why should you now

109th Chorus

"Was it a bright afternoon,
    bright with seeing?"
Asks the literary type
    sitting in a chair
In an afternoon's dream
And you see his buddy comin in,
Holding his coat to the hook
After closing the door,
You see it on a Thurber Cartoon,
In New Yorker, the funny
Fat figures V-cut and Z-cut
In squares, spilling cartons
of spaghetti to their orb ball
OON LINE ANOON
    POP CLOUD - WORD - HOLE
And people thumb thru
      Reg'ally
And up comes the laugh, the yok,
      Funny Thurber
      Cartoon there,
    "Was it a bright afternoon,
bright with seeing?"
        looking over his newspaper
        or poetry pad

110th Chorus

I know how to withstand poison
And sickness known to man,
In this void. I'm no apprentice
When it comes to remembering
The eternity of suffering
Quietly I've been through,
Without complaint, sensing inside
Pain the gloriful um mystery.
Afternoons as a kid I'd listen
to radio programs for to see
the scratch between announcements,
Knowing the invalid is glad
only because he's mad
enough to appreciate every
little thing that blazons there
in the swarmstorm of his eye
Transcendental Inner Mind
where glorious radiant Howdahs
are being carried by elephants
through groves of flowing milk
past paradises of waterfall
into the valley of bright gems
be rubying an antique ocean
floor of undiscovered splendor
in the heart of unhappiness

111th Chorus

I didnt attain nothin
When I attained Highest
        Perfect
        Wisdom
      Known in Sanskrit as
      Anuttara Samyak Sambodhi

I attained absolutely nothing,
Nothing came over me,
    nothing was realizable —

In dropping all false conceptions
    of anything at all
I even dropped my conception
    of highest old wisdom
And turned to the world,
    a Buddha inside,
And said nothing.

People asked me questions
about tomatos robbing the vine
and rotting on the vine
and I had no idea
what I was thinking about

    and abided
    in blank ecstasy

112th Chorus

Dont sound reasonable,
      dont sound possible,
            when you bring it up
But if you dont bring it up,
            everything is alright.
Dont believe Mr. Believe Me?
Dont think about him
            and boy
                  you'll see how he vanishes
                  in morning's mist
                  when the moon
                  is a crescent a banana
                  and birds jump
and far over the Atlantic
where Red Amida is Shining
you'll hear the Call Trumpet
of East is Alright with the West
In the Orb of the Womb
            of Tathagata
                  so round
                  so empty
            so unbelievably
                  false-lyingly
            empty of persimonny

113th Chorus

Got up and dressed up
    and went out & got laid
Then died and got buried
    in a coffin in the grave,
Man —
    Yet everything is perfect,
Because it is empty,
Because it is perfect
    with emptiness,
Because it's not even happening.

Everything
Is Ignorant of its own emptiness —
Anger
Doesnt like to be reminded of fits —

You start with the Teaching
    Inscrutable of the Diamond
And end with it, your goal
    is your startingplace,
No race was run, no walk
    of prophetic toenails
Across Arabies of hot
    meaning — you just
    numbly dont get there

114th Chorus

Everything is perfect, dear friend.
When you wrote the letter
I was writing you one,
I checked on the dates,
Just about right, and One.

You dont have to worry
        about colics & fits
From me any more
        or evermore either

You dont have to worry bout death.
Everything you do, is like your hero
The Sweetest angelic tenor of man
Wailing sweet bop
On a front afternoon
When not leading the band
And every note plaintive,
Every note Call for Loss
        of our Love and Mastery —
        just so, eternalized —

You are a great man
I've gone inside myself
And there to find you
        And little ants too

115th Chorus

LANGUID JUNKEY SPEECH WITH LIDDED EYES
So bleakly junk hit me never.
Must be something wrong with the day.
"How you feel?" — "Um — Ow" —
Green is the wainscot, wait
For the vaquero, 1, 2, 3 —
  all the faces of man
  are torting on one
  neck

Lousy feeling of never-get-high,
I could swallow a bomb
And sit there a-sighing,
T's a Baudelairean day,
Nothing goes right — millions
Of dollars of letters from home
And the feeling of being,
Ordinary, sane, sight —
  Arm muscles are tense
  Nothing ever right
You cant feel right
  Hung in Partiality
   For to feel the unconditional
   No-term ecstasy
   Where, of nothing,
    I mean, of nothing,
    That would be best

116th Chorus

The Jews Wrote American Music

    Niki Niki Niki- la
    Che wa miena
        Pee tee Wah

Song of Lil Mexico Children

    Kitchi Kitchi
      Kitchy val

Big fat mustachio'd businessmen
Have just to finish their commercial
And go home, saw em at five
Drinking beer at Bar's Alive
While old Canuck Pot
  Looked white & cold
  In corner, countin candles

       Music

It's an Aztec Radio
    with the sounds thick & guttural
    kicking out of the teeth
The Great Jazz Singer
    was Jolson the Vaudeville Singer?
No, and not Miles, me.

117th Chorus

Me, Paraclete, you. Ye —
Me, Paraclete, Thee —
Thou Maitreya Love of the Future
— Me.
    Me Santiveda me, saint,
  Me sinner me — Me baptist
  A-traptist of Lower
         Absafactus

Me — You
Me, alone in understandin old
    void of I love you,
    feel fine

Me, you gotta love yourself,
    love, somethin,
    thass all I can say

The witchcraft Indiana girls
    that didnt sing with their hearts,
    where never in a better
    shock of hay hocks
    than the oldtime
    singer with dusty feet
    that chased death
    comes and enfolds you

118th Chorus

It's all the same to me.
The radio I dont wanta hear
And cant have to hear
Plays one thing and another
Of great Sarah Vag

      but no I stop
      and grasp
      and I forget
      that it's my own fault

See how you do it?

      And having grasped
      go on singing
         because I wouldnt
           be writing these poems
           if I didnt know

That I grasp I sing

I've had times of no-singing,
   they were the same

Music is noise, Poetry dirt

119th Chorus

Self be your lantern,
Self be your guide —
Thus Spake Tathagata
Warning of radios
That would come
Some day
And make people
Listen to automatic
Words of others

and the general flash of noises,
forgetting self, not-self —
Forgetting the secret . . .

Up on high in the mountains so high
the high magic priests are
swabbing in the deck
of broken rib torsos
cracked in the rack
of
Kallaquack
tryin to figure yr way
outa the calamity of dust and
eternity, buz, you better
get on back to your kind
b o a t

120th Chorus

Junkies that get too high
Shoot up their old stock of stuff
And sit stupidly on edge
Of bed nodding over
The single sentence in the paper
   They been staring at all night —
   Six, seven hours they'll do this,
   Or get hungup on paragraphs:

"You go on the nod,
    Then you come up,
       Then you start readin
          it again
      Then you go on the nod again
    and everytime you read it
         it gets better"

    You dont remember the next
        rebirth
      but you remember
      the experience

"Took me all evening to read
3 or 4 pages, ossified,
on the nod"

121st Chorus

Everything is in the same moment
It doesnt matter how much money you have
It's happening feebly now,
    the works
I can taste the uneaten food
    I'll find
In the next city
    in this dream

I can feel the iron railroads
    like marshmallow

I cant tell the difference
    between mental and real

It's all happening
It wont end
It'll be good
The money that was to have been spent
    on the backward nations
of the world, has already been
    spent in Forward Time

Forward to the Sea,
    and the Sea Comes back to you
    and there's no escaping
    when you're a fish
    the nets of summer destiny

122nd Chorus

We cannot break
Something that doesnt exist

Derange pas ta tendresse,
Dont break your tenderness

Is advice that comes to "me"

What a poem the knowledge
    that Time
With its Pasts & Presents
    & Appurtenant
Futures, is One Thing
THE THING ONE WHOLE MASS
Getting dimmer and dimmer
       to the feel

What glorious repose knowing
What a Golden Age
    of Silent Darkness
    in my Happy Heart
    as I lay contemplating
    the fact that I shall die
    anyhow regardless of race
    regardless of grace

123rd Chorus

The essence is realizable in words
That fade as they approach.
What's to be done Bodhisattva?
O live quietly; live to love
Everybody.
   Be devout under trees
   At midnight on the ground.
        No hope in a room
        of dispelling the gloom
        that's assembled
        Since Moses

Life is the same as death
But the soul continues
In the same blinding light.
   Eating is the same as Not Eating
   But the stomach continues,
   The thinking goes on.

You've got to stop thinking,
   stop breathing.
How can you travel from Muzzy
          to
        Muzzy?
   Forgive everyone for yr own sins
   And be sure to tell them
You love them which you do

124th Chorus

The tall thin rawboned fellow
Come up to Paw and me
On the misty racetrack.
"Got a good one in the fourth."
"How do YOU know"
        says my Dad
"I'm a jockey"
His hat waved over his eyes
In the rain.
I saw Arkansaw
behind him.
He looked too big to be a jockey
        to me —
"Just put 4 dollars to win
And give me half
        the winnings."
I dont remember now
        whether my father fell
And got laid by that line,
    But "too big
            man
            he too big
            to be a jockey"
            was my thought

125th Chorus

He shoulda been a football coach,
Joe McCarthy — the guy
that was a turncoat
at the assistant editor
of the Daily Worker?
— the tenement marble
sculptured Attican column
in the moonlight illuminating
my eyes — the ross
osh dewey bilbo long
scatter de crash talk
of Fascist BWAS!
— CLAP TRAP
the machinegunners of Goa
are in the Street mashing
the Saints of McCarthy
Cohn Captus & Company
and all I gotta say is,
remove my name
       from the list
  And Buddha's too
Buddha's me, in the list,
      no-name.

126th Chorus

Like running a stick thru water
The use and effect
Of tellin people that
                    their house
                 is burning,
And that the Buddha, an old
           And wise father
Will save them by holy
             subterfuge,

Crying: "Out, out, little ones,
The fire will burn you!
I promise to give you fine
                          carts
Three in number, different,
Charming, the goat cart,
The deer cart, and
The cart of the bullock

Gayly bedecked — With oranges,
Flowers, holy maidens & trees,"
So the children rush out, saved,
   And he gives them
   The incomparable single Greatcart
   Of the White Bullock, all snow.

127th Chorus

Nobody knows the other side
    of my house,
My corner where I was born,
    dusty guitars
Of my tired little street where
    with little feet
I beetled and I wheedled
    with my sisters
And waited for afternoon sunfall
    call a kids
And ma's to bring me back
    to supper mainline
Hum washing line tortillas
    and beans,
That Honey Pure land,
    of Mominu,
Where I lived a myriad
    kotis of millions
Of incalculable
    be-aeons ago
When white while joyous
    was also
Center of lake of light

128th Chorus

How solid our ignorance —
how empty our substance

and the conscience
keeps bleeding

and decay is slow —
children grow.

The toothbone goes
Out of mushy pulp
And you cry
As if rocks
Had been dumped
From a truck
On your back
And whimper,
    saying
      'O Lord,
    Mercy on Mission.'

129th Chorus

We've all been sent
On a mission
To conquer the desert
So that the Shrouded
    Traveller
Behind us
Makes tracks in the dust
  that dont exist,
    He'll, or We'll,
      All end in Hell
      All end in Heaven
      For sure —
Unless my guess is wrong,
We are all in for it
And our time
Is Life,
The Penalty,
      Death.
    The Reward
    To the Victor
    Then Goes.
The Victor is Not Self

130th Chorus

And the Victor is Not Pride
And the Victor is not.
   Thus Spake Tathagata

     But I get tired
     Of waiting in pain
     In a situation
     Where I aint sure.

Where I am not sure
Where I am Wolfe
   Sorrow
   Whitman Free
   Melville dark
   Mark Twain Mark
    Twain
     where I am
      w i l d
Where I am M i l d

131st Chorus

Where I aim
And do not Miss

Dawdlers.
    Alla them are dawdlers.
Poets.
    Call themselves poets
Call themselves Kings
    Call themselves Free
Calls themself
    Hennis free
Calls themself
Calls themself
    Calls themself catshit
    Calls themself mean
    Calls themself me

132nd Chorus

Innumeral infinite songs.
Great suffering of the atomic
     in verse
Which may or not be
     controlled
  By a consciousness
  Of which you & the
ripples of the waves
   are a part.
      That's Buddhism.
      That's Universal Mind

      Pan Cosmodicy

      Einstein believed
      In the God of Spinoza

(— Two Jews
 — Two Frenchmen)

133rd Chorus

"Einstein probably put a lot
of people in the bughouse by
saying that

All those pseudo intellectuals
went home & read Spinoza
then they dig in
to the subtleties
of Pantheism —
    After 10 years of research
    they wrap it up
    & sit down on a bench
    & decide to forget
    all about it.

Because Pantheism's
Too Much for Em.

    They wind up trying to
find out Plato, Aristotle,
    they end up in a
    vicious Morphine circle"

134th Chorus

"The only cure for
       morphine poisoning
Is more morphine."

This is the real morphine.

Now it's after supper
And the little kids
Are out on the street
Yelling "Mo perro,
Mo perro, mo perro"
And the sky is purple
In old hazish Mexico
of Hashisch, Shaslik
And Veal Parmezan.

Russian Spy Buses
       Tooting
       "Salud"

135th Chorus

The ants are gone asleep
By now, out on those plains
Of pulque and rice
Beyond Pascual
And the Cactus Town
   Matador pan
   Pazatza cuaro
   Mix-technique
   Poop
   Indio
      Yo yo catlepol
      Moon Yowl
      Indian
      Town & City

Vendors of Take a Giant Step
Say Hailé
In back se malleys
Selling drunks

136th Chorus

I always did say
Aunt Semonila
The Amapola Champeen
Of Yon Yucatan
will never find
   her potatoes
    Till she sticks in her hands

Potatoes of paternity
Grow deep,
     Edie.

Nut went Crazy
Fife Faces of Man
In One Cell
Ow are you?
   Fall.

137th Chorus

AZTEC BLUES
"A kek Horrac"
I hear in the Aztec Night
Of Mystery
Where the Plateau Moon
With Moon Citlapol
Over the dobe roofs
Of Heroé Mexico.
" S c r e e a a - ra - sarat"
The Scraping of Chair,
Followed by Toot & Boom.
   Punk! says Iron Pot Lid.
   Tup! says finger toilet.
   Tuck! says dime on Ice.
   Ferwutl says Beard Bird.
Howl of Moondogs in Monterrey
When dry is Riverbottom
Baseball Rock
Nothing nada like this scene
Of Apish majesty
In April's hide of hair

138th Chorus

It's really a Brooklyn Night
    the Aztec Night
  the Mix Toltec Night
  the Saragossa Night
  the Tarasco Night

  Jaqui Keracky
  Grow Opium
  In Ole Culiacan

       (BLANK, the singer
           sings nothing)

139th Chorus

I said Well
Bad time of month for me —
So last I saw or heard a
    him —
  Matter of fact, he even —
  But he never hardly
    gave me the 10 pesos

So I was figuring it was
    worthwhile to keep
    the bum outa my hair,
    ten pesos

Only one guy I ever known
He always paid me back
Angel Gabriel
Bright on High

140th Chorus

Fifty pesos

3 Cheers Forever
It's beautiful to be comfortable
Nirvana here I am

When I was born Tathagatas
Assembled from all universes
And chanted in my ear
The gray song of Nirvana
  Saying "Dont Come Back"
    Then my Angel Gerard
    Protected & comforted me
    In the Rainy Misery
    And my mother smiled
    And my father was dark
    And my sister
    And I sat on the floor
    And I Void Listened
    To the Eternal Return
    With no Expression

141st Chorus

Zoom
S t a r
of Holy
I n d i a n
N I G H T

The Tathata
of
Eminence
is
Silence

The Clear Sight
of Varied Crystal
Shining Mountains
shifting in the Air

Exploding Snow

is Transcendental
Brilliant Shattered
Hammered Smithy
Emerald Green
Rubioso Mostofo
Be spark snaked

142nd Chorus

Muck Ruby
Crystal Set
Smithereen
Holylilypad
Bean —
A la Pieté —

Truss in dental
Pop Oly Ruby
Tobby Tun w d l
1 x t s 8 7 r e r (

Gainesville Georgia — Sleeping in the
grass on a July night —
Dream of climbing night bank
behind the Joe Louis signatures
    We die with same
    unconcern we live

143rd Chorus

(pause)

Junkies
Should be practical nurses
And be given permits
To get 3 to 5 grains a day
Every day,
The older addicts need more.
    Drug Addicts
    Are human beings
    Less dangerous
    Than alcoholics

    And alcoholics arent so bad
Look at the speed drivers
Look at the sex fiends

144th Chorus

Look at the sex fiends
Speeding thru their suicide!
  Nembutols!
  Guns & jumps in the river!
  Lilly saved the man's life!
    Flying with legs
    out the window
      to crash the locomotive
      at the X Crossing

    X!

I been in crashes,
I been in many a bad night,
I been in Nova Scotia
Investigating the Blight.
  And Bright the Vast
    Atlantic Greenland
    Mountain cap
    Of Old Atombomb
    Atlantis

145th Chorus

A BANG OF M
A razor mountain —
An Empire State Building
    needle Hypo —
A boiling cauldron
    cucharra —
A sneeze, a wheeze —
            A Cough
A cotton sucking —
    A Bang of M
Anticommunism is an
    arbitrary distinction
Depending on Communism
    A shoot-in
    Pull out needle

James Huneker
Alfred Knopf
H L Mencken
Edgar Lee Masters

146th Chorus

The Big Engines
In the night —
The Diesel on the Pass,
The Airplane in the Pan
    American night —
Night —

The Blazing Silence in the Night,
    the Pan Canadian Night —
The Eagle on the Pass,
    the Wire on the Rail,
the High Hot Iron
    of my heart.

The blazing chickaball
    Whap-by
Extry special Super
    High Job
Ole 169 be
    floundering
Down to Kill Roy

147th Chorus

The Sock
 Wock Williby
  Balloons
In the shitfence

The Angels
 in Heaven
  I knew

The Angel in Heaven
 Gabriel Toot Boy
 Horn n All
 Blows Awful
 Blues When
 Toy Doy
 Done Bo Moy
 From China mo Moy
 To Ole Penoy,
  Oy — y —
 Y gerta
  was gordo

148th Chorus

Instrucciones
Precaucion

Whichever way you look
        you're looking East

Same with West

Whichever etc. way you look,
        you're looking West

Thus Spake Tathagata

In the Eastern Heavens I knew
Blue Auroras of the new
Most of David ever knew
Find the Bible Desert,
Rock,
    Ti Jean Picotée
    Silence
        Bzzzzz
      the razor in-cut
      of void meat

149th Chorus

I keep falling in love
     with my mother,
I dont want to hurt her
— Of all people to hurt.

Every time I see her
     she's grown older
But her uniform always
     amazes me
For its Dutch simplicity
And the Doll she is,
The doll-like way
     she stands
Bowlegged in my dreams,
Waiting to serve me.

     And I am only an Apache
     Smoking Hashi
     In old Cabashy
     By the Lamp

150th Chorus

Appeasement is Hypnotism
When the Houri Indian
    snakecharmer gets under way
        swaying his crock toilet
        picoloette clarinoot
        at the snake's bony
        leer
              he is leading a band
              like Sammy Kaye
              that could erupt
              and kill him

The Weasels Wait

If Buddha appeased
    the Likhavi Tribesmen
It means he must have hypnotized
    and pleased
Their appeasable hearts
    with talk
Of Grand Nirvana's
Holy Paradise

151st Chorus

STILL LIFE
A candle dripped all its
    gysm
To the bottom of a strawberry
    designed
Mexican Beer tray —
    A single edge razorblade,
    Partially underneath
    The blade of a butter knife
    Abstracted from old
            camp
            packs —

And a tin cup.

This is the Matisse Story
Of a simple arrangement
Of natural objects
In a room on a Sunday
Afternoon —
        bits of dry dust,
        black ashes

152nd Chorus

The edge of the tray
    is bright red —
The strawberries are crimson
    dull painted
    juicy dimensional
    indefinable silver lights
    on the knife & blade
    brass dark death
    and the tragic gloom
    inside the lull
    of the tumbled wax
    Attican and Shapely

The rim sadness aluminum
    ALCO Shipwave
    cup —

Then, in real life not
    still life — comes
    the filthy dry gray
    ash tray of butts
    and matchlet tips

153rd Chorus

Sir Garver is cleaning
His Attic and Castle,
Sniffing & snappin
The Bardic Be
    Garters —
Wearing the huge shroud
    sorcerer's head
Picking up deadbeats
    Offa his bed.
Tucking the sheets in
    of no consequence;
Turning and struggling
    to kneel to a stand
Off the bed of dimensions
    & middles
And spans,
    that wont let him lie
        straight
    In the South American
    Pan

154th Chorus

Pan mattress, pan spang,
      pan bang,
Perdoneme, pardon
        me.

He's got a rich cover
Lines made of wine
To cover his bed with
And pull in the line

And unties his bow strings
Of bathrobe & gore,
His plue pajamas
  Poaping
        around all that
        gore
    His feet clean & shiny
    Like askin for more

155th Chorus

And as he keeps washing
    & blowing his poor nose
And waiting for death
    to make V-repose
Out of hands he now rubs with
    the towel of More.

Coffee cup's a-covered
    Friend does the Sneeze
Death'll overcome him
    in Some Fleece of Sleep

Nirvana is Snowing
Right down on his head
Everything's all right
In Heaven in High
Inside this blue bottle
    us flies rage & wait
But outside is the Rosy
    of Purple O Gate
    O J O

156th Chorus

I know we're all straight
I knew from a tree
I leaned on a tree
And the tree told me

Tree told me Haby
The Maybe is Abey,
The Kapey is Correcty,
You'll be allarighty

Trees dont talk good
No they don't talk good
This tree just told me
  See Eternity
  Is the other side
  Of the other part
  Of your mind
  That you ignore
  Because you want to

157th Chorus

The Art of Kindness
Is a dream
That was foretold by prophets
Of Old, wd. be continuous
With no broken lines
Buddha after Buddha
Crashing in from Heavens
    Farther than expressioning,
Bringing the Single Teaching:
    Love Everywhere.

Bring on the single teaching,
It's all indeed in Love;
Love not of Loved Object
Cause no object exists,
Love of Objectlessness,
When nothing exists
Save yourself and your not-self
Hung in a Moon
Of Perfect O Canopy
Sorrowing Starborrowing
    Happiness Parade

158th Chorus

It wont happen is what
    it is —
It'll lose touch —
     It was the same in past
               eternities

     It will be with the bees
     now

      the feeling of in and out
      your feeling of being alive
      is the feeling of in & out
      your feeling of being dead
         u n a l i v e

When it comes you wont
    sneeze no more, Gesundheit.

It wont happen, is what
    is —
    And
    it aint happenin now

Smile & think deeply

159th Chorus

Blook Bleak.
Bleak was Blook,
    an Onionchaser Hen
    necked Glutinous
    Huge Food monster
    that you ate
    with FLAN & Syrup
    in a sticky universe

Blook on the Mountaintop,
    Bleak;
Blake by the Mountainside,
    Baah! —
Boom went the Crasher
    Mountain Heidi
    Kerplunk Archagelan
    Swiss Funnel
    Top of Funny Ships
    Singing & sinking
    In a Glutinous Sea
    (of Lese Majesty.)

160th Chorus

Poppa told me a perfect pome.
It's simple
The smiles of hungry sexy
     brunettes
Looking to lock you in
     lock joint and all
And those eyes of Italian
     deep scenery
In Riviera's of Caviar
     Tree
And Mulberry Bee
     Lampshade
     Sun Ahmenides
     Ahmenemet!
     Ak!
       That's your rosy
        Figury,
           another word
              for future —
That's your come itself

161st Chorus

It's a starry disaster
Wobbling many times
Like Sick-to-my-Stomach
The All Slop of Brothers,
Every word that Pegler utters,
"So-pa-top-a-ta!"
Shout children on street —
("Luz!" is her call name)
Horn of Sunday car, yar
Of yak-pass mufflerless
Cars — "You writing that down?
"Not necessarily in agreement
With general trend against
The labor movement" — but here's
his takeoff on Eleanor
Roosevelt 'This is My Day,'
It's a funny statement —
Pegler took out My Day
And rolled into thought
Tortilla & puts it on one
　　　　article —
　　　　(con salsa —)

162nd Chorus

BILL'S DREAMS
Slim girls in thin kimonos
Of blue silk, thin gossamer,
Long, that you could see thru,
Lying down, half-sitting,
Smoking through long tubes
In which every once in a while
An attendant places drug,
In a central bowl,
   And as they smoke on
   An attendant sprinkles
   their eyes with talcum
      powder
And they flutter their eyes
To the joy of it.
     Then, back in the Tombs,
      He's smoking in his cell
      And the smoke became
      Singing people fading
      And coming with smoke
      and a guy passing bread
       Passes him up —

163rd Chorus

Left the Tombs to go
  and look at the
  Millions of cut glass —
— a guy clocking them,
as you look you swallow,
you get so fat
you can't leave the building,
— stand straight,
dont tip over, breathe
in such a way yr fatness
deflates, go back to
          the Tombs,
ride the elevator —
          he tips over again,
gazes on the Lights,
eats them, is clocked,
   gets so fat
      he cant leave elevator,
has to stand straight
and breathe out the fat —
— hurry back to the Tombs

164th Chorus

Grand Central Station,
   side entrance
   where they unload produce

— He & friends get scraps
   of meat & cabbage,
All starving,
   on floor are iron plates
   hot, not too hot,
They all start slowly
   cooking, but keep moving up
   as men with central
   hotplate heat
   get impatient & eat
   meat half raw —
   so he keeps pushing up
   his little meat
   towards the center —
These people are all bums —
Hang around in restaurants
Where there's nothing to eat
And you sit a table
And suddenly there's a guy

165th Chorus

under the table
cooking your leg
in some kind of steam
— much quicker job
with the steam on the leg
than central radiant
wildheat of cabbage
            plates
        in Grand C Station

And I see: "Everybody's eatin you.
You eat them,
makes no difference,
the essence does not pass
From mouth to mouth
And craw to craw,
it's ignorance does.
        ignorant form.
        the essence is not
            disturbed
            really,
    Like the sudden thought
    of India is a dream"

166th Chorus

A home for unmarried fathers.

He said I must investigate
   some day, that —
Homefront married fathers,
— some whacky idea —
like a home for unmarried fathers
   would be.
Pegler and the Cabinet
  of Peligroso FDR
   — Firstbase, Perkins;
    Eleanor, Right field;
    Pitching, Cervantes
    the Cuban Newcomer
    from downriver
    Harlem
       riding a white
       horse riot
       Picasso
       in his helmet
       Jesus

167th Chorus

The details are all the same,
Like honey stored in beehives,
Like atomic power, so many
Atoms, the details per
Square inch are the life of it
And the death of it
   The critical mass collapses
   And like a tumbled Sand castle
   When the tide of disintegration
   And its conception rise,
     Flops into the sea softmaw
     Sand salvaging, bells
     Toll it not offshore.
     The Castle was a Dream.
       Now learn
       that the water is a dream
       For when the Tide of Disaster
       Rises water will disintegrate
       And all will be left
       Is the Successful Savior
       Abiding Everywhere in
       Beginningless Ecstatic Nobody

168th Chorus

Asking questions and listening
        is sincerity;
Asking questions and listening
        without really listening
Is a kind of sincerity; but
Talking about yourself alla
        time, is not insincere.

It's all the same thing
In the long run, the short run
        the no run

Whitman examined grass
        and concluded
It to be the genesis
        & juice, of pretty girls.

"Hair of Graves," footsteps
Of Lost Children,
Forgotten park meadows,
— Looking over your shoulder
        At the beautiful maidens —

169th Chorus

Lie down
 Rest
  Breathe slowly

Dead in Time
You're dead already
What's a little bit more time got to do
       with it
So you're dead
So the Living Loathe the Dead,
 themselves —
So forgive, reassure, pat, protect,
 and purify them
 Whatever way is best.
   Thus Spake, Tathagata.

The girls are pretty
But their cherries are itty

And if they aint got cherries
 Sleep in the Park anyway

And if you dont go near them
You dont get that sensation
Of their inexhaustible delicacy

Dead in Time — Rest in Time

170th Chorus

Rest in Delicacy
The far border of the puff lace
    clouds of Amida's Western
    Heaven of Diamond Repose
    is Delicate

And delicate is the Spanish
    language, delicate the Spanish
    they speak in Upper Bleak
    where King Sariputra
    holds forth a tablet of ice
    (I mean diamonds)
    to be read by the highest
    most delicate Bodhi papa
    in the whole confraternity
    — Old Buddha of Old
    In his Magic Selves
    Commingled as One, Maitri,
    Coos delicate songs
    To the lyres & guitars
    Of the minds of the Lapis
    Lazuli old Saints

171st Chorus

When I hear that serenade
    in blue —
Tell me darling are these things
    the same
That we had always known
    Well all alone
And true, it's that serenade
    O serenade,
In the blue, in the blue.

Oopli da da
Aow dee a dee e-da-ha
    You never had no chance
    Fate dealt you wrong hands

Romance never came back

Crashing interruptions
        So I'm with you
      happy once again
     and singing all my blues
   in tune with you
       with you

172nd Chorus

When I hear that
      serenade in bleu,

  OO dee de ree,
      — a song I could sing
      in a low new voice
      to be recorded
      on quiet microphones
      of the Roman Afternoon,
      tape, a new kind of voice,
      sung for the self
      sung for yourself
      to hear in a room
      where you dont
      want to be
      interrupt
      ed

Or made to sing dirges
Of suicide & main
in the candle of the handle
of the coffin to blame

173rd Chorus

The funerals of the doornails
Gay Chocolateers with sadness
    of Marshes across
    their Germany
Hope of Eleanoras of Russia
    rising from
    the railroad
    Nevsky track
Loud upturned chocolate bedpans
    of Saturday Night
    Drugstore Windows
    showing rubber
    and the sexfiend
    watching
Oldtime childhood shoesheens
The Music of the uninhabited spheres
    being played & developed
    over ages for no one
That's the Radio to me
The Ultimo Actual Soundbody
    discriminating in the air
    by means of men tubes
    invented by the 95 devils

174th Chorus

The freshwater eels of Europe
That climb up their rivers
And presumably raid fjords
And eat up pools, curious
Proustian visitors from up the
                           mountain
Of the sea, which, when they die,
they re-cross, to Bermuda,
from whence they came, to die.

Must be that these eel
Have a yen to explore
The veins of Old Atlantis
From their sunken mountaintop
This side Canaryas
But no — they slide
From Europe to Ukraine
And down the Belgian Rivers,
And blankly in the void
Swim back to spawn
And die with longfaced pouts
— Poor fish.

175th Chorus

Cunalingus
My sister's playin piana in Vienna
The Jews are Genius Gypsies
The Moors are Poor.
Aristotle, Isabel,
Ferdinand the Bull.

Ferdinand was no Dumb-Bell —
Piano high was Vienna
When Freud interviewed
    The oversexed Rothschilds
    And Richjews of Vienna
    And the Gypsies were camped
    In apartments — with lamps —

All the wealth of Europe
        had poured
Into Vienna — Freud was there —
So his Psychoanalysis Sex
Chart of Mad talk
Was accepted as Gospel
By undermined golfcourses
            of the River West —
The multiple too-much of the world

176th Chorus

The reason why there are so many things
Is because the mind breaks it up,
The shapes are empty
That sprung into come
But the mind wont know this
Till a Buddha with golden
Lighted finger, hath pointed
   To the thumb, & made an aphorism
   In a robe on the street,
   That you'll know what it means
   For there to be too many things
   In a world of no-thing.

      One no-thing
      Equals
      All things

When sad sick women
Sing their sex blues
In yr ear, have no fear
   have no fear —
  the moon is true, enough,
  but, but, but, but, but,
  it keeps adding up

177th Chorus

Farewell, tendril

I dont wanta play like that
　　when I find you
　　as a world
　　In my heart
　　I dont want
　　To talk it lightly
　　And make jokes
　　And find myself
　　Paranoically
　　Grunting loud huge grunt
　　Of Gordo Exer-
　　Indian-Cise,
　　　　I'd — O Christ —
　　　　wouldn't want to be cool
　　　　in hot hell
　　　　and be goofing
　　　　when yr sweet attentions
　　　　all me, thee,
　　　　describe, self-descried
　　　　in one essential
　　　　　　l i g h t ,
　　　　the holy gold so-called

178th Chorus

Put the blame on intelligence —
    the reason, no,
    not the bloody reason,
    the asskissed burned
    Chicago Putdown
    talk of time —
who was it maimed
    the rescue,
and made — the mistake —
        and held
        the loft
        and lost
        and got lost
        and knew nothing —

What knew the blame?
Who put the blame?
Who's trying to throw me
                        out?

Who am I?
do I exist?
    (I don't even exist anyhow)

179th Chorus

Glenn Miller and I were heroes
When it was discovered
That I was the most beautiful
Boy of my generation,
They told Glenn Miller,
Whereby he got inspired
And wrote the saxophone
Wrote the reed sections —
like sautergain & finn —
and then they all did dance
and kissed me mooning stars
and I became the Yokum
of the wall-gang, flowers,
and believed in truth & loved
the snowy earth
    and had no truck
    and no responsibility

a bhikku in my heart
waiting for philosophy's
    dreadful murderer
       B U D D H A

180th Chorus

When you work on that railroad
You gotta know what old boy's
                              sayin
In that en-gyne,
      When you head brakie
      just showin up for work
      on a cold mist dusk
      ready to roll
      to on down the line
      lettuce fields
      of Elkhorn
      & sea-marshes
      of the hobo highriding
      night, flash Salinas —

"Somebody asked me where
          I come from
I tell them it's none a their
                              business,
      Cincinnatta"—

      Poetry just doesnt get there

181st Chorus

The girls go for that long red
                                    tongue,
From the pimp with the long red
                                    car,
They lay it in his hand
The profits' curfew
He takes it "The Yellow Kid"
— He's the Man —

She goes home and hustles,
Remembering Caroline,
The hills when little
      The raw logcabin
          rotting in the piney woods
          where the mule was mush
    and pup-dog howled
          for no owner
          all one owl-hoot night
          and watermelon flies
          on the porch

But she love that long red tongue

          And the Man
          is a Sucker

"SOMEONE LOWER THAN SHE IS"

182nd Chorus

The Essence of Existence
    is Buddhahood —
As a Buddha
    you know
    that all the sounds
    that wave from a tree
    and the sights
    from a sea of fairies
        in Isles of Blest
    and all the tastes
        in Nectar Soup
    and all the odors
        in rose arbour
    — ah rose, July rose —
        bee-dead rose —

and all the feelings
    in the titwillow's
    chuckling throat
and all the thoughts
    in the raggedy mop
    of the brain —
    one dinner

183rd Chorus

"Only awake to Universal Mind
And realize that there is nothing
Whatever to be attained. This
Is the real Buddha."

Thus spake Hsi Yun
      to P'ei Hsiu

Names so much like each other
You know it cant be wrong
You know that sweet Hsi Yun
Had eyes to see the Karma
Wobbling in the balloon
— shiney —
      millions of dollars damage
      from rains and floods —
vast fading centers of a Kansas
      central standard time

        buss-i-ness
        my fron

Only awake to Universal Mind,
      accept everything,
      see everything,
      it is empty,
Accept as thus — the Truth.

184th Chorus

"Men are afraid to forget
  their own minds,
Fearing to fall thru the void
With nothing to which they can cling.

They do not know
  that the void
  is not really void
  but the real realm
  of the Dharma"—

Wow, I thought reading that,
  when I start falling
  in that inhuman pit
  of dizzy death
  I'll know (if
  smart enough t'remember)
  that all the black
  tunnels of hate
  or love I'm falling
  through, are
   really radiant
  right eternities
    for me

185th Chorus

Farewell, pistil —
    "as old as space"
    "without the faintest tendency
    towards rebirth"

No-self, no-self, no-self,
Dass iss the order of the day,
Virya, Zeal, Wednesday,
When I can turn this old
    patayo Matago dun's
    nest of hornet toad
    shoot bewallopers
    worrying in Finnegan's
    Whorehouse about nothing,
    into a Pagoda of Bright
      Jesus Lace Snow
      Japana dreams,
      with showers of aura
      arras flower rose
      bepetalling pet by pet
      from the holy dispenser
      of dogs —
          Farewell, puppy

186th Chorus

It's all happening in snow
But I shudder.
    Now there's no reason for that.
    Now argue the sky saints.
    And down below, I mourn
        and low like an old cow
        in a rastro slaughterhouse
        in the I-Dont-Know
        district of Hellavides'
        Devil Dang —
        No, hmf, damn, boy,
        boom — hell's clutters
        that meated dante
        when he virgilized
        his poign —
            bom —
                om, atva,
                svaha, snatva,
        Holy Old Howl Who'll
            Ya
            Is Okay

187th Chorus

Do not Seek,
          and Eliminate nothing,
          concluded the Chinese
          Master of 840 B.C.

"Observe the Void which lies
          before your eyes
          How can you set about
                    eliminating it?"

Buddhism is a big bomb on the head
     and it hurts

After which comes I know
          the milky fliss,
fluff, soft AW eternities,
          skyrockets,
snowflakes, hope revealed,
          snow
Gerard, Pa, lamb,
          Sax,
Heaven, you, me.

·188th Chorus

And tonight I'll pray
    And O I'll call Fugen
    and Kwannon to my aid
    and ask them to let me
    hear their transcendental
    silence sound,
                    learning
                    thereby
                    Fugen
                    Avaloki-
                    tesvara'an
                    mostafokas
                    fakirs, makers,
                sing sound silence
                of my sound

O bless me, make me safe,
    say, 'No-Yo' but save
    'Me no?' save
        No-me — I beseech
        save no-me

189th Chorus

Petronic, Satiricon —
The Black Mass is the Christian
Devil Mass
    "A guy in there
    gives a supper
    and has his funeral oration
    spoken, & coffin bared
    in which he is to lie,
    all dishes are black,
    all food black & white
    (that which can be)
    — they have world-food
    at this banquet of death,
    the wealthy man celebrant
    says he'll die early
    and violently"
        and Does he?

Petronius Arbitum —
    elegant queer,
        my dear

190th Chorus

What I have attained in Buddhism
    is nothing.
What I wish to attain,
    is nothing.

Let me explain.
In perceiving the Dharma
    I achieved nothing —
What worries me is not
    nothing
But everything, the trouble is
    number,
But since everything is nothing
    then I am worried nil.
In seeking to attain the Dharma
    I failed, attaining nothing,
And so I succeeded the goal,
Which was, pure happy
    nothing.
No matter how you cut it
    it's empty delightful boloney

191st Chorus

My startingplace and my goal
are right here in this simple
                    space hole

Sings Shinran:—
"All that have obstructions
Are not impeded
By the Clouds of Light."

It is like the Iddhi Magic
Mentioned in Surangama Sutra,
Where say, The Bhikshu
Who delights in Transcendental
Solitude and Brilliant Silence
And Rhinoceros Sorrow
Shall be saved, & transported
    Magically in the air
    To his Blessed Pure Land
    Diamond Irradiation
    From the Crown of Buddha.
    Wild — I wait by candlelight
        for confirmation
        (And I see waving whitenesses)

192nd Chorus

"O thou who holdest the seal
    of power, raise thy diamond
    hand, bring to naught, destroy,
    exterminate.

O thou sustainer, sustain
    all who are in extremity.

O thou purifier, purify all
    who are in bondage to self.

May the ender of suffering
    be victorious. Om!

Om! Oh! Thou perfectly enlightened,
    enlighten all sentient beings.
O thou who art perfect in wisdom
    and compassion,
Emancipate all beings, & bring
    them to Buddhahood. Om!

Adoration to Tathagata (Attainer
    to Actual Isness), Sugata
    (Attainer to Actual Goodness),
    Buddha (Who is Awake), Perfect
    in Pity and Intelligence

193rd Chorus

Who has accomplished,
And is accomplishing,
And will accomplish,
All these words
Of mystery,
Svaha,
So be it,
Amen."

Numberless roses arranged,
The milk of merriment
    without the curds,
The Pleased Milk
    of Humankindness
The Frowns of worried saints,
The Helpless Hands of Buddha
    burning,
The Crown Prince of the Lotus
    Blossom Sky,
Lover of all the mental phantoms
    in the mind —
Wordmaker, curdmaker
    Kingmaker, Ding
Dong, the Buddha's Gong

194th Chorus

Being in selfless one-ness
With the such-ness
That is Tathagatahood,
So is everybody else
Lost with you
In that bright sea
Of non-personality.

In teaching the Paramitas
Of Virtue and Sweetness,
The Wu-Weis of Love,
The Tehs of Sensibility,
And all the Tibetan Arhat
Secrets of the Buddha Mountain
World up & down of which
We race in celestial racingcars
On imaginary hills seeking
Salvation at the goal,
    Flagged by Dominos of Bodhi
    And Oil men Ragged Hero
        Mechanic Sariputran
    Minnesinging Gurus, on we rave.

195th Chorus

The songs that erupt
Are gist of the poesy,
Come by themselves, hark,
Stark as prisoners in a cave
Let out to sunlight, ragged
And beautiful when you look close
And see underneath the beards
the holy blue eyes of humanity
And brown.

The stars on high sing
songs of their own, in motion
that doesnt move, real,
Unreal, singsong, spheres:—

But human poetries
    With God as their design
        Sing with another law
            Of spheres & ensigns
                And rip me a blues,
                Son, blow me a bop,
                Let me hear 'bout heaven
                In Brass Fluglemop

196th Chorus

So I write about heaven,
Smoke for the scene,
Wanta bring everyone
Straight to the dream.

If you only could hold
      what you know
As you know it forever,
      instead-a
Moving from griefy to griefy,
      lament to lament,
Groan, and have to come out
      and smile once again,
— S teada all that,
A hospital for the sick,
Lying high in crystal,
In heaven of pure
      adamantine
Consanguine
Partiality devoid
Of conditions, free —
      Here I go rowin
      Thru Lake Innifree
      Looking for Nirvana
      Inside me

197th Chorus

Inside, Inside Me,
I'se free
Free as the bee
Inside he.
    Lord have a mercy
    on Hallelujah Town
I got to stomp my foot,
And say, whee,
    hey dad, now oan,
    from now oan,
    I dont wanta
    cant wanta
    wont wanta
      hear about it
not in my Oakland
    Saloon, not in my bar
    Not in my brokenglass
    Not in my jar

    Blue, black, race, grace,
        face,
    I love ye.

198th Chorus

Nirvana aint inside me
    cause there aint no me.

Nirvana's everywhere
    'xceptin' what's everywhere
And so all is nowhere.

    Swimmin free, in the lake free,
    Rowing to the other beachy.

    Tall guards you say? tall
      saloons? maloons?
    Tall goons? Tall tunes?

        Tall stately heroes
        Tall calm saints
        Tall long tendrils
          of cloud-air
        Tall unobstructed
          ghost whitenesses
        Imagining on the edge
          of the pier —
        Just not there.

199th Chorus

Empty balloons of gorgeous?
Wild upskies bedazzling radiant?
Immense arcades of secret joy?
Caves of light, Ya-Vingo,
    dream-material palaces
    high in the texture
      of the high thought?

Nirvana? Heaven?
    X? Whatyoucallit?

S w e a r

Huge milky areas of silence
Permeated by rose petals
crushed in diamond vats —
Great baths of glory? —
Singing quiet humsound?
White light of black eternity?
    Golden Secret Figures
    Of Unimaginable
    Inexpressible Flowers
    Blooming in the One Own
      Mind
      Essence

200th Chorus

White figures throughout
    made of light,
Like a truck becomes a square
    mass of shining light bars,
Empty Apparitional secret
    figure of the mind.
More than that. Face
    is mass of swarm-roe
    starlight, insanity
    itself personified
    & taking up space
    & penetrable throughout.

Secret parleys with saviour
Angels outside brown rooms
Where phantoms converge
In light, black and white,
Dazzling in the middle
With one Insane Bar Light —
    One Shiningness
And you know darkness nullifies
    the color
    Into Nirvana No

201st Chorus

When the girls start puttin
   Nirvana-No on their lips
Nobody'll see them.
   Poor girls, did they always
Want attention? Did they
   always disturb
The sitting saint in the woods
   and make him feel
Cheap by sayin: "Those
   guys think they
can sit down & be God."
— "They think they dont
   have to work
   because they are God
   and they sit down
   and think they are God"
   — Those Guys . . .
Over their heads is the unbelievable
               unending
               emptiness
               the enormous
               nothingness
               of the skies

     And they claim

202nd Chorus

A white poem, a white pure
    spotless poem
A bright poem
A nothing poem
A no-poem non poem
    nondream clean
    silverdawn clear
    silent of birds
    pool-burble-bark
            clear
        the lark of trees
        the needle pines
            the rock the pool
                the sandy shore
    the cleanness of dogs
            the
            frogs
            the
        pure white
        spotless
        Honen
    Honey Land
        Blues

203rd Chorus

Heaven's inside you but there's no you.
What does that mean?
    said the teacher,
  The Great Holy the All Holy
    Old Teacher:—

All you've got to do
Everytime you feel sick
Is stop (this madhouse
        shot of yours
        is not exactly
        the immemorial miel)

      stop — and stare
          through the things
          before your eyes
          with eyes unfocused
          and as soon as they move
          you will have seen
          that they move
          to illusion.

Seeing that all's illusion
You lose your mind
In meditation
And heal yourself well
    (AND WHAT'S BEEN HEALED?)

204th Chorus

What's been buried in the grave?
   Dust.
Perfect dust?
    Perfect dust in time.
  Time.
     Time is dust.
     Time's not dust
     Time's already happened
         immemorially
     The pearl of the gods
     the agonizer of Wests
     The ball in the bubble
        void

    Time —
       Dont worry bout time.

What's been buried inside me
    for sure?
The substance of my own father's
    empty light
Derived from time working
    on dirt
And clay bones.
       Buddha's River.

205th Chorus

Enter the Holy Stream.
March with the Saints.
Follow along the emptiness.
Follow bright the ferrymen
And follow the All Star
And sing with the others
In praise of the light
In praise of the emptiness
     so bright
In praise of the OO-LA-LA'S
Of Parisian Women.

In praise of the singsong
    mingsong
    brokesong
    lostsong
      Ah Time
        Ah Perturbable

      Me, Sir,
Dis-beturbable Ameget
      Me

206th Chorus

Maaaaaah! said the sheep
And opened its foxtail soft
Mouth to say something empty,
To express its reverentation,

And M n a a a came
        the bull cry something-cry
Because you cant sing
        open yr mouth with poems
        without you make sound
        and sound is wrong
                sound is noise
    But only human speech
        and also all sentient
        communication
        pointing to the finger
        that points at sound
        saying 'Sound is Noise' —
        Otherwise
                sound itself
                un-self-enlightenable
                would go on blatting
                & blaring unrecognized
                as emptiness and silence

207th Chorus

Aztec Blues — Imitation of Pound
A God called "Drink the Flood
     Water" — HUETEOTL —
Is a very old God.
What older God could you get
    GLED-ZAL-WAD-LE,
    The Sound of the Feathered Serpent,
    cause of the flood.
    He came from:
    "Destroyed-Over-Flooded-Land-
      Exiled-Him-Water-Pour,"
    Which means: He is Water.
        He is the Flood.
        He is the Ocean that Floods

Serpent as the Sign of Flood, Ah
                Sax —

Bird-feather is a sign of escape,
flight, exile —
    The Feathered Serpent
    Snakes that Fly
    Nail Eternity
    To bye/
    TONA TI UH:- "Of the Sunken Your Ear"

208th Chorus

Anciently in cities
    men have been sitting
    in waiting rooms
    in the night bloated
    with food and alcohol
    waiting waiting waiting
    as though the city existed not.
They are so old.
    They think all alike.
        I've seen them die in chairs
        Quietly in cities they never planned.
        Seen them sing in saloons
        For muffled uproars.
        Seen men in coffee houses
        Shoot the opium cup
        With Greeks of Brotherhood.
        Aztec Pulque Distributors
        Rembrandtian city committees
        And unions of Masons —
Shoot the sperm cup to me, Jim,
These partitioned Anglo Spanese
Singing sneerers perturbing
You in the background
Are your father's kindly
        buriers

209th Chorus

Well, that about does me in.
I've packed my bags and time
Has come to start to heaven.
Afraid of the trip. Always
Thought it was short & snappy
And I wouldnt worry. Or
Always thought I'd be glad to go.
  But who's glad to go? I want gold.
  I want rich safety in my legs
  And good bones made of empty milk
  Of God-Kindness — I want
  I need I cry like baby
  I want my Partotooty
  Sweety backpie back
  And dong strang bang bong
  Dont scrounge my yoll-scrolls
  And try to fool with me
  One more time & I report you
  To the pimp, whore God —
        I got the woozes
        Said the wrong thing
        Want gold want gold
        Gold of eternity

210th Chorus

Impressionism. The drowned afternoon
   along the sunny carnival —
Trees waving over rock walls
   of drowned scummers —
Glutted bloatbellies blue as the bay
   scummed in tangle raft —
Shit on a leaf, by the pier,
   shit used as leaf paper
Piled by flooded Ack Merrimoil
      the Plantaneous River
      of Fra Devilico Mojostico
      the Funny Folly Phoney balloon
      of Polateira Mia OOLA
      the Crap' in-ping, Caing,
      and mutter of imbecile
      boys in jungle beehive fish.
         Blop.
   Centurions. Potalishakions.
   Prerts. F. Funks. P.l.u.p.s.
   Frains Trails Moss.
         Scum. Sing my lil yella
         basket. A tisket. Tasket.
         Athabasket. Ma the basket.

211th Chorus

The wheel of the quivering meat
                                        conception
Turns in the void expelling human beings,
Pigs, turtles, frogs, insects, nits,
Mice, lice, lizards, rats, roan
Racinghorses, poxy bucolic pigtics,
Horrible unnameable lice of vultures,
Murderous attacking dog-armies
Of Africa, Rhinos roaming in the
                                        jungle,
Vast boars and huge gigantic bull
Elephants, rams, eagles, condors,
Pones and Porcupines and Pills —
All the endless conception of living
                                        beings
Gnashing everywhere in Consciousness
Throughout the ten directions of space
Occupying all the quarters in & out,
From supermicroscopic no-bug
To huge Galaxy Lightyear Bowell
Illuminating the sky of one Mind —
        Poor! I wish I was free
        of that slaving meat wheel
        and safe in heaven dead

212th Chorus

All of this meat is in dreadful pain
Anytime circumstances attain
To its attention like a servant
And pricking goads invest the flesh,
And it quivers, meat, & owner cries
And wishes "Why was I born with a body,
Why do I have this painful hive
   Of hope-of-honey-milk yet bane
   Of bitterest reward, as if, to wish
   For flesh was sin alone itself — ?"
And now you gotta pay, rhinoceros
               and you,
   Tho his hide's toughern ten young men
Armed with picks against the Grim
                  Reaper
Whose scythe is preceded by pitchforks
Of temptation & hell, the Horror:
   "Think of pain, you're being hurt,
   Hurry, hurry, think of pain
   Before they make a fool of you
   And discover that you dont feel
   It's the best possible privilege
   To be alive just to die
   And die in denizen of misery"

213th Chorus

Poem dedicated to Allen Ginsberg
— prap — rot — rort —
mort — port — lort — snort
— pell mell — rhine wine —
roll royce — ring ming —
mock my lot — roll my doll —
pull my hairline — smell my kell —
wail my siren — pile my ane —
loose my shoetongue — sing my aim —
loll my wildmoll — roll my
                          luck —
lay my cashier gone amuk —
suck my lamppole, raise the bane,
              hang the traitor
              inside my brain
        Fill my pail well,
ding my bell, smile for the ladies,
              come from hell

214th Chorus

Ling the long Chinese peeswallower,
  a lad like ye,
Laid his hand on Garty's knee
  and paid the pree —

Shong the mong of anisfore,
    Maharajah
Dusty, kinked the from of Jaidphur
    from the Konk mirror free
So all Bojangles Banghard
    had to do
Was roil his rolly tooty
    mot the polyong,
And if you knew what I meant
  you would say
You disgust me —

Aright, ring the devil free —
    Bong — Ring the devil free
    Prong — ring the devil free,
    Song, ring the devil free,
  Ong, ring the biney free

215th Chorus

Moll the mingling, mixup
All your mixupery,
And mail it in one envelopey:
Propey, Slopey, Kree.
Motey, slottey, notty,
Potty, shotty, rotty, wotty,
Salty, grainy, wavey,
Takey, Carey, Andy
Sari Pari Avi Ava
Gava lava mava dava
Sava wava ga-ha-va
Graharva pharva
Dharma rikey rokkkk
Tokkkk sokkkk
M r o c k k , the Org
Of Old Pootatolato
England Ireland
O
Sail to Sea

216th-A Chorus

Fuck, I'm tired of this imagery
— I wanta quit this horseshit
    go home
    and go to bed

But I got no home,
      sickabed,
        suckatootle,
          wanta led
          bonda londa
          rolla molla
        sick to my
          bella bella
          donna donna
          I'm a goner
          Soner, loner,
          moaner,
            Poan, cornbelly,
            No loan,
              Ai, ack,
        Crack /

I'm sick of this
misery poesy/ flap Jean
               Louis
               Miseree

216th-B Chorus

Filling the air with an arbitrary dream —
When no desire arises, that is the original
Feeling of peace in Actual Nature —
It is not moot to question how a dream
                                        ends
Whenaslong as it ends —
A Baby in Pain:
      tell the proud seminal mother
      how many more of that she wants
      to satisfy her fertile ego
      and how many more babies
      crying in the night, angry screech,
      knowing that their flesh is on the block
      of death the hungry butcher.
      — how many pigs hung upsidedown
         and slowly bled to death
         by reverent ritual fools
         with no noses and no eyes

Emancipate the human masses
Of this world from slavery to life
And death, by abolishing death
And exterminating birth —
      O Samson me that —
The Venerable Kerouac, friend of Cows
DEPEND ON VAST MOTIONLESS THOUGHT

216th-C Chorus

Well roofed pleasant little hut,
    screened from winds:
That's all I need. Foursquare
The image of the Buddha in my brain,
Drawing from the countryside the verdant
Fantasm of conception, saying:
"We green imageries of bush & tree,
Like you, have risen from a mystery,
And the mystery is fantastic,
Unreal, illusion, and sane,
And strange — It is: When ye
Are not born, thou never showest:
When thou art born thou showest,
Thou showest emeralds and pine trees
And thou showest, and if not born
Thou showest naught in white
Dazzling buried in mindless obscure sea
That strange eternity devises to befool,
Befoul and play unfair with Mag
The worshipper and worrier, Man,
Mag, Mad,
        it's all green trees, men
        And dogs of toothbone:
        All shine in the dust,
        All the same Novice Scotia"

217th Chorus

Sooladat smarty pines came prappin down
My line of least regard last Prapopooty
And whattaya think Old Father Time
made him? a western sponnet
Without no false on bonnet,
Trap in the cock adus time of the Nigh,
Slight the leak of recompense being
                              hermasodized
By finey wild traphoods in all
                    their estapular
                    glories
Gleaming their shining-rising spears
        against the High Thap All Thup —
So I aim my gazoota always
        to the God, remembering the origin
Of all beasts and cod, Bostonian
By nature, with no minda my own,
Could write about railroads, quietus
These blues, hurt my hand more,
    Rack my hand with labor of nada
    — Run 100 yard dash
      in Ole Ensanada —
S what'll have to do,
        this gin & tonics
Perss o monnix
        twab
        twab
        twabble
        all day

218th Chorus

Sight the saver having from the coast
   put further items down — what? you
   wish to talk to me, hear me scratch
   at the mean little door, hiding in my bonnet —
O come off it, the vast canopial
Assemblies wait for yr honest spontaneous reply.
      What shall it be?
      I promise to reject pain when next
      My turn comes back again
      I promise not to steal, nor go to hell
      For stealing
      I promise to say Na
      When Tathagata's Angels
      Ride for me. Na —
      I wanta go to Inside-Me,
      Is there such a place? No is.
   Flap the wack I smack the hydrant
of desire, sip sop the twill —
        (hiding all them guys — 'twere
      as I told you, old dreams
        of young brides'll do you no more good)
Wake up Scribe! Pharisee!
  The a x x a b a t a
  f l O R I A N I O L A
  S P R I N G   T I M E
    OW OH ALL
    OFFICIAL SEMINARY

219th Chorus

Saints, I give myself up to thee.
Thou hast me. What mayest thou do?
What hast thou? Hast nothing?
Hast illusion. Hast rage, regret,
Hast pain. Pain wont be found
Outside the Monastery only —
      Hast decaying saints like Purushka
      Magnificent Russian-booted bird loving
      Father Zossima under the cross
      In his father cell in Holy Russia
      And Alyosha falls to the ground
      And Weeps, as Rakitin smears.
      Grushenka sits him on her lap
      And lacky daisies him to lull
      And love and loll with her
      And wild he runs home in the night
      Over Charade Chagall fences
            snow-white
      To the pink cow of his father's ear,
      Which he slits, presenting to Ivan
      As an intellectual courtesy, Dmitri
      Burps, Smerdyakov smirks.
      The Devil giggles in his poorclothes.
Saints, accept me to the drama
of thy faithful desire.
No me? No drama to desire?
No Alyosha, no Russia, no tears?
Good good good good, my saints.
No saints? No no no my saints.
No no? No such thing as no.

220th Chorus

Pieces of precious emerald and jade
Come from igneous rock once on fire,
Erupted through a volcano, sandstone,
Came out oozing in crevices
Pieces of light long buried in the earth
Are diamonds and floods of them.
"Amen the Jewel in the Lotus!"
Prays the Tibetan Saint with Prayerwheel,
"Om Mani Padhme Hum,"
He wants to pile up credit
Like the jewel in the rock
So that when he's found
The doves will have laid aground
Eggs of bright amethystine
Wallowing splendorous decay,
Kings of Ore, art of fathers
Handed to sons, fire and air.
Kingdoms have been founded on diamonds,
Emeralds and pearls, and walkways
Of padded lily milky meshed
And crushed in holy feet, Maha
Graha Sattva, Being of Great Power,
Fortunes in Wisdom, Stores of Love.
    Mountains rise high, diamonds shine,
    Men ride high the alumpshine
        The lump sunshine
        Delicious is the taste of Porcupine

221st Chorus

Old Man Mose
Early American Jazz pianist
Had a grandson
Called Deadbelly.
Old Man Mose walloped
    the rollickin keyport
    Wahoo wildhouse Piany
    with monkies in his hair
    drooling spaghetti, beer
    and beans, with a cigar
    mashed in his countenance
    of gleaming happiness
    the furtive madman
    of old sane times.

Deadbelly dont hide it —
    Lead killed Leadbelly —
Deadbelly admit
    Deadbelly modern cat
Cool — Deadbelly, Man,
Craziest.
        Old Man Mose is Dead
        But Deadbelly get Ahead
        Ha ha ha

222nd Chorus

Mexico Camera
I'm walkin down Orizaba Street
looking everywhere. Ahead of me I
see a mansion, with wall, big
lawn, Spanish interiors, fancy
windows very impressive

Further bloated copulated bloats

Silent separative furniture
   The Story of No-Mad, silent
      separative corpses;
     Ignorino the Indian General
      He Chief, wow,
      Of Southern Sonora,
       You know the Bum,
       what was his name?
     Asserfelter Shnard Marade,
     the Marauding Hightailer
       of Southern Slopetawvia,
       krum, full of kerrs and kierke
                  gaard/
      and bash bah
       the P l a p

223rd Chorus

Pineys hursaphies,
    Finally allawies,
        Fonally finalles.
Hookies from OO-SKOOL,
    Polls for Who Hook Fish,
        Fowl for Fair Weather.
Wu! cries the Indian Boy
    in the South Sampan Night,
"Esta que ferro," you be of iron,
I'll be a damn tootely wow
    wot Rot Moongut Rise Shine
    Hogwater Wheel —
        Juice a the eel —
    In Old Lake Miel —
        Honey wheel —
Sound
    E Terpt T A pt T E rt W —
    Song of I Snug Our Song
        Sang of Asia High Gang
        Clang of Iron O Hell Pot —
        Spert of Ole Watson Ville
        Gert —
        Smert —
        Noise of old sad so
        Such Is
Sing a little ditty of the moon inside the loony
boon of snow white blooms in Parkadystan
       I S T A M H O W   H U C K

224th Chorus

Great God Amighty
    What's to be done?
    O what's to be done?
Sings the majestical keener
    and moaner
At the Mexican Funeral home —
And from a clap in the upclouds
Comes a clap of clouts,
"All has been done."
As Theravada say "Nothing"
Nada moonshine number, whats been done?
All been done — all singly blessed —
    All has been done? The mansion's
    been built and Damema
    grown old & died
        in burning house within?
    And Seventeen Sutras & Lotuses
    Transmitted by Perfumed Hand
    From Jingle to Jiggle
    The Hip Hou Parade
        of Togas & Mowrdogrogas
    Of Maharajah India —
        'All's been done'
           'so rest'
        Repose yourself

225th Chorus

The void that's highly embraceable
    during sleep
Has no location and no fret;
Yet I keep restless mental searching
And geographical meandering
To find the Holy Inside Milk
Damema gave to all.

Damema, Mother of Buddhas,
    Mother of Milk

In the dark I wryly remonstrate
With my sillier self
For feigning to believe
In the reality of anything
Especially the so-called reality
Of giving the Discipline
The full desert-hut workout
And superman solitude
And continual enlightened trance
With no cares in the open
And no walls closing in
The Bright Internal Heaven
Of the Starry Night
Of the Cloud Mopped afternoon —
    Oh, Ah, Gold, Honey,
    I've lost my way.

226th Chorus

There is no Way to lose.
If there was a way,
        then,
                when sun is shining on pond
                and I go West, thou East,
                which one does the true sun
                follow?
                which one does the true one
                borrow?
                since neither one is the true one,
                there is no true one way.
                And the sun is the delusion
                Of a way multiplied by two
                And multiplied millionfold.
Since there is no Way, no Buddhas,
No Dharmas, no Conceptions,
Only One Ecstasy —
                And Right Mindfulness
                Is mindfulness that the way is No-Way —
                        Anyhow Sameway —
Then what am I to do
                Beyond writing this instructing
                Poesy, ride a magic carpet
                Of self ecstasy, or wait
                For death like the children
                In the Funeral Street after
                The black bus has departed —
                Or — what?

227th Chorus

Merde and misery,
I'm completely in pain
Waiting without mercy
For the worst to happen.
I'm completely at a loss,
    There is no hope
Though I know the arbitrary conception
    of suffering is racking
    my metaphysical
    handicapped ribs,
    and I dont even exist less sing,
    and I been paid
    for work I done
    when I was young
    and work was fun
    and I dont know name from mercy,
    aint got no blues
    no shoes no eyes
    no shoetongues, lungs,
    no happiness, no art,
    nothing to do, nothin to part,
    no hairs to split
    sidewalks to spit,
    words to make flit
    in the fun-of make-it,
        horror & makeshift poetry
        covering the fact I'm afraid
        to work at a steady job
    jungles of hair on my wrists
    magnified 1000 times
        in Hells of Eternity

228th Chorus

Praised be man, he is existing in milk
    and living in lillies —
And his violin music takes place in milk
    and creamy emptiness —
Praised be the unfolded inside petal
    flesh of tend'rest thought —
      (petrels on the follying
      wave-valleys idly
      sing themselves asleep) —
Praised be delusion, the ripple —
Praised the Holy Ocean of Eternity —
Praised be I, writing, dead already &
    dead again —
   Dipped in ancid inkl
          the flamd
          of T i m
   the Anglo Oglo Saxon Maneuvers
Of Old Poet-o's —
      Praised be wood, it is milk —
      Praised be Honey at the Source —
Praised be the embrace of soft sleep
— the valor of angels in valleys
    of hell on earth below —
Praised be the Non ending —
Praised be the lights of earth-man —
Praised be the watchers —
     Praised be my fellow man
     For dwelling in milk

229th Chorus

In the ocean there's a very sad turtle
(Even tho the SS *Mainline* Fishin Ship
    is reeling in the merit like mad)
Swims longmouthed & sad, looking
    for the Impossible Except Once
    afternoon when the Yoke, Oh,
    the old Buddha Yoke set a-floatin
    is in the water where the turtle raises
    his be-watery snop to the sea
    and the Yoke yokes the Turtle
        a Eternity —
"Tell me O Bhikkus,
      what are the chances,
        of such a happening,
          for the turtle is old
            and the yoke free,
            and the 7 oceans bigger
              than any we see
              in this tiny party."
Chances are slender —
    In a million million billion kotis
    of Aeons and Incalculables, Yes,
    the Turtle will set that Yoke free,
    but till then, harder yet
    are the chances, for a man
    to be reborn a man
    in this Karma earth

230th Chorus

Love's multitudinous boneyard
    of decay,
The spilled milk of heroes,
Destruction of silk kerchiefs
    by dust storm,
Caress of heroes blindfolded to posts,
Murder victims admitted to this life,
Skeletons bartering fingers and joints,
The quivering meat of the elephants of kindness
    being torn apart by vultures,
Conceptions of delicate kneecaps,
Fear of rats dripping with bacteria,
Golgotha Cold Hope for Gold Hope,
Damp leaves of Autumn against
    the wood of boats,
Seahorse's delicate imagery of glue,
Sentimental "I Love You" no more,
Death by long exposure to defilement,
Frightening ravishing mysterious beings
    concealing their sex,
Pieces of the Buddha-material frozen
    and sliced microscopically
In Morgues of the North,
Penis apples going to seed,
The severed gullets more numerous than sands —
      Like kissing my kitten in the belly
      The softness of our reward

231st Chorus

Dead and dont know it,
    Living and do.

The living have a dead idea.

A person is a living idea;
    after death, a dead idea.

The idea of living is the same
    as the idea of death.

The dead have a living idea —
Dead, it aint my fault
    I was only an idea —

Respected penitence in a shack
    dedicated to the study of Origin —

The good Buddha-material
    is not a sin-cloth —
Cloth of Light —
Beings alive indicate death
    by their jaunty work
Just as the dead indicate the living
    by their silence
        When rock becomes air
    I will be there

232nd Chorus

Buddhists are the only people who dont lie,
In the Sacred Diamond Sutra
Mention is made that God will die —
    "There are no Buddhas
    and no Dharmas" — means —
    There is no Universal Salvation Self,
    The Tathagata of Thusness has understood
    His own Luvaic Emanations
    As being empty, himself and his womb
    Included — No Self God Heaven
    Where we all meet and make it,
    But the Meltingplace of the Bone Entire
    In One Light of Mahayana Gold,
    Asvhaghosha's singing in your ear,
    And Jesus at your feet, washing them,
    And St. Francis whistling for the birds —
    All conjoined though and melted
    And all be-forgotten, pas't on,
    Come into Change's Lightless Domain
    And beyond all Conception,
    Waiting in anticipatory halls
    Of Bar-Light, ranging, searchlights
    Of the Eye, Maitreya and his love,
    The dazzling obscure parade
    of elemental diamond phantoms
    And dominos of chance,
    Skeletons painted on Negresses
    Standing by unimportant-to-you
    Doorways, into Sleep-With-Me
    The alley way behind.

233rd Chorus

There is no selfhood that can begin the practice
Of seeking to attain Anuttara Samyak Sambodhi
Highest Perfect Wisdom
    Yet
  "Faithfully and earnestly observe and study
  and explain this Scripture to others"
      is the gory reminder of bone.
      Others. "Listen, Subhuti! Wherever
      This Scripture shall be observed and studied
      and explained, that place
      will become sacred ground
      to which countless devas and angels
      will bring offerings. Such
      places, however humble they may be,
      will be reverenced as though
      they were famous temples & pagodas,
      to which countless pilgrims will come
      to offer worship and incense.
      And over them the devas & angels
      Will hover like a cloud & will sprinkle
      offerings of celestial flowers
      upon them."

    The Pilgrims are happy.

The Pilgrim of the Holy Grail, the Snail,
The Pilgrim of the Fine Pagoda,
The Pilgrim of the Five Tendencies
    to Hear and Support Prayer —

No selfhood that can begin the practice
      of seeking to attain

234th Chorus

Holy poetry.
    "All things are empty of self-marks."
    "If it is space
        that is perception of sight
    You ought to know,
        and if we were to substitute
    One for the other, who'd win?"
        Santiveda, St. Francis, A Kempis,
        Hara

A sinner may go to Heaven
    by serving God as a sinner

235th Chorus

Dont camp,
You know very well
    What'll happen to you
When you die
    and claim
        you dont know you're dead
        when you die and you know
        "I know dont know that I'm dead"

Dont camp. Death, the no-buzz,
    no-voices, is, must be, the same,
    as life, the tzirripirrit of thupsounds
    in this crazy world that horrifies my mornings
    and makes me mad wildhaired in a room
    like old metaphysical ogrish poets
    in rooms of macabre mysteries.

But it's hard to pretend you dont know
That when you die you wont know.

I know that I'm dead.
I wont camp. I'm dead now.
What am I waiting for to vanish?
    The dead dont vanish?
        Go up in dirt?
    How do I know that I'm dead.
        Because I'm alive
        and I got work to do
        Oh me, Oh my,
           Hello — Come in —

237

236th Chorus

The Buddhist Saints are the incomparable saints
Mooing continue of lovemilk, mewling
And purling with lovely voices for love,
For perfect compassionate pity
Without making one false move
                         of action,
Perfectly accommodating commiserations
For all sentient belaboring things.
      Passive Sweetsaints
      Waiting for yr Holyhood,
      Hoping your eventual join
      In their bright confraternity.

Perfect Divines. I can name some.
What's in a name. They were saints
Of the Religion of the Awakening
From the Dream of Existence
And non-existence.
      They know that life and death,
      The knowing of life, muteness of death,
      Are mutual dual twin opposites
      Conceptioning on each side of the Truth
      Which is the pivot in the Center
      And which says: "Neither life
      nor death — neither existence
      nor non-existence — but the central
      lapse and absence of them both
      (in Love's Holy Void Abode)"

237th Chorus

"Ma mère, tu est la terre."
What does that mean?
For one thing, Damema was the mother of Buddhas,
   in Ancient India and Modern Asia
   you put up a Virgin Mary very weird
   in your altars and ikons, Damema,
   with crowns of light coming out of her head
   and lotuses and incense sticks
   and big sad blue eyes inside Flowers.

People light perpetual candles to her name,
Wax in glass with wick, fire,
For 30 days the pale Mystic Face
Of Damema flickers in the ceiling corner
And the dogs bark outside.
      They get water from the moon,
      Send boys out of sight in baskets,
      Sleep in the streets of night,
      Playing flutes & having curbstone nightclubs
      And the curbstone put there by the British —
      They honor and beseech and pray to
           Damema.

To me Damema is like Virgin Mary,
Mother Maya of Siddhartha Buddha
Died at his childbirth,
Like all mothers should be,
Going to heaven on their impulse
   Pure and free and champion of birth.
      Damema the Milky Mother
      Damema the Secret Hero

238th Chorus

Who was it wrote "Money is the root of all evil?"
Was it Oscar Wilde in one of his witties?
Was it Celine — nah.
Was it Alexander Pope, Benjamin Franklin
    or William Shakespeare —
Was it Pope in one of his many
    clever lines?
Benjamin in his Almanac of Peers
    has Richard the Chicken Liver
    Express a private pear.

Or is Shakespeare blowing wild
Confucius-Polonius witticismical
Paternity-type advice —
"Money is the root of all evil"
For I will
Write
In my will
"I regret that 1 was not able
To love money more."
For which reason I go into retreat
And monastery — all monastic in a cell
With devotions and hellpellmell
And Yumas Arctic Gizoto Almanac
Priotho Consumas Konas
    In the Corner, & Mother Damema

239th Chorus

Charley Parker Looked like Buddha
Charley Parker, who recently died
Laughing at a juggler on the TV
after weeks of strain and sickness,
was called the Perfect Musician.
And his expression on his face
Was as calm, beautiful, and profound
As the image of the Buddha
Represented in the East, the lidded eyes,
The expression that says "All is Well"
— This was what Charley Parker
Said when he played, All is Well.
You had the feeling of early-in-the-morning
Like a hermit's joy, or like
                    the perfect cry
Of some wild gang at a jam session
"Wail, Wop" — Charley burst
His lungs to reach the speed
Of what the speedsters wanted
And what they wanted
Was his Eternal Slowdown.
A great musician and a great
                    creator of forms
That ultimately find expression
In mores and what have you.

240th Chorus

Musically as important as Beethoven,
Yet not regarded as such at all,
A genteel conductor of string
                orchestras
In front of which he stood,
Proud and calm, like a leader
                of music
In the Great Historic World Night,
And wailed his little saxophone,
The alto, with piercing clear
                lament
In perfect tune & shining harmony,
Toot — as listeners reacted
Without showing it, and began talking
And soon the whole joint is rocking
And everybody talking and Charley
                Parker
Whistling them on to the brink of eternity
With his Irish St Patrick
                patootle stick,
And like the holy piss we blop
And we plop in the waters of
                slaughter
And white meat, and die
One after one, in time.

241st Chorus

And how sweet a story it is
When you hear Charley Parker
               tell it,
Either on records or at sessions,
Or at official bits in clubs,
Shots in the arm for the wallet,
Gleefully he Whistled the
                       perfect
                       horn

Anyhow, made no difference.

Charley Parker, forgive me —
Forgive me for not answering your eyes —
For not having made an indication
Of that which you can devise —
Charley Parker, pray for me —
Pray for me and everybody
In the Nirvanas of your brain
Where you hide, indulgent and huge,
No longer Charley Parker
But the secret unsayable name
That carries with it merit
Not to be measured from here
To up, down, east, or west —
— Charley Parker, lay the bane,
   off me, and every body

242nd Chorus

The sound in your mind
  is the first sound
    that you could sing

If you were singing
  at a cash register
    with nothing on yr mind —

But when that grim reper
  comes to lay you
    look out my lady

He will steal all you got
  while you dingle with the dangle
  and having robbed you

Vanish.
  Which will be your best reward,
  T'were better to get rid o
  John O' Twill, then sit a-mortying
  In this Half Eternity with nobody
  To save the old man being hanged
  In my closet for nothing
  And everybody watches
  When the act is done —

Stop the murder and the suicide!
  All's well!
    I am the Guard